MAMA'S MEMOIRS:

GROWING UP IN THE
SANTA CRUZ MOUNTAINS

Highland Grammar School, the class of 1902.

Cover Photo — Emma Bessie Ingraham, taken some time shortly before her marriage to Adolph Rapp.

Photo from Previous Page — Highland Grammar School, Class of 1902. Back row: Emma Ingraham (Mama) at center, the teacher is far right. Second top row: fourth and fifth from left are Mildred and Esther Jones. Front row: Belle Ingraham, second from right. The other children are unidentifiable. The dog's name was Jumbo.

DEDICATION

In memory of Mama. This book, I hope, will complete the circle.

"Mama's Memoirs: Growing up in the Santa Cruz Mountains"
by Margaret Louise Rapp Tarquinio, 1926-1994
edited and designed by J. Alex Tarquinio,
with additional research by the editor.

Published by Vista Del Mar Press
24900 Highland Way, Ste. 501
Los Gatos, CA 95030

First Edition

International Standard Book Number: 9648618-0-1

Library of Congress Catalog Card Number: 95-90729

The following photos were provided courtesey of:
Emma Mae Lydon, pages 27, 47, 119 and 127
Ruth and Esther Jaun, pages 83 and 205
Adolph Rapp, Jr., page 216
UCSC Special Collections, pages 29, 132, 150 and 153
All other photos are from the author's private collection.
The issue of J.J. (Joseph) Bamber's *The Realty*,
on page 64, is also from the author's private collection.

The maps and diagrams on pages 24, 61, 62, 84, 96, 237 and
pages 268-275 were designed by the editor,
based on sketches by the author;
except the maps on pages 24 and 96, which were
based on sketches by Emma Mae Lydon;
and the diagram on page 84, which is
based on information provided by Ruth and Esther Jaun.

NOTES

For historical purposes, every effort has been made to use the real name of each individual in this book. All stories are as accurate as legends can be.

All letters are copied as they were written, misspellings and all. The author feels this adds to the flavor of the times.

MAMA'S MEMOIRS:

GROWING UP IN THE SANTA CRUZ MOUNTAINS

BY MARGARET LOUISE RAPP TARQUINIO

EDITED BY J. ALEX TARQUINIO

VISTA DEL MAR PRESS

LOS GATOS, CALIF.

1995

TABLE OF CONTENTS

PREFACE

This book is in memory of my mother, Emma Bessie Ingraham Rapp, who would have been one hundred and one years old on August 9, 1989. She lived from August 9, 1888 to August 8, 1975.

This book had a long gestation period. For most of my adult life, I thought that Mama's stories should be written down. Then in May of 1989, I took a train trip across the states with my daughter-in-law Norma and my grandson, Andy. As we were crossing Iowa, I told them the story of my great-grandparents settling there in 1854.

My daughter, Janet, joined us in Pennsylvania, where we were visiting my husband's relatives for a few days. Norma and Andy flew back to California and Janet and I went on to New York City, where she now lives.

I told Janet some of Mama's old stories that the train trip across the states had reminded me of. Suddenly the idea struck me to write Mama's stories down myself. I was in a writing frenzy during the rest of my stay in New York, sometimes staying up all night to write.

A month later, Janet and I boarded another cross country train, this time to Everett, Washington. We spent a couple of weeks with my son Steve and his wife Cheryl, who live in Arlington. My husband, Amadeus, planned to join us two weeks later, so we had a lot of time on our hands and no wheels of our own. This inspired Janet to get out her word processor, which we had lugged across the country in a big brown box, transfering it between trains in Chicago and sleeping with it under our feet at night.

Janet is a playwright, and also earns her living doing word processing. She volunteered to help me with the typing and the story editing. We worked ten or twelve hours a day in Arlington, and continued throughout the summer after returning to San Jose. We talked with many of our relatives, and also interviewed old neighbors who still live in the Santa Cruz Mountains.

This book has been written with the hope of capturing some of Mama's incredible stories about growing up in the Santa Cruz Mountains while there are still some people alive who remember her. It is true what they say, that everyone is still alive until the last person who remembers them is gone. Hopefully with this book, Mama, her stories, and some of her valuable wisdom will live on and on.

Margaret Louise Rapp Tarquinio
San Jose, California
1989

FOREWORD

My mother titled the final chapter of her book "The Last Story." But it just wasn't so. Many untold stories still lurk in the twists and turns of Longridge Road. Later in her life, my mother could still surprise me with a new one now and again, one she thought I must have heard by then.

And then there was my mother, who, like her mother, lived to become a legend of Longridge. My grandmother became something of a local historian simply by outliving the other pioneers to the area. She spun her yarns about the old days well into the 1970s, for anyone who cared to listen. My mother had the vision and the perseverance to record these stories for anyone in future generations who cares to listen.

The initial phase of this project began as she described it in her preface of 1989. We put in a lot of work over the summer on this book. Then for about six months afterwards, she finished writing it and xeroxed numerous copies for friends and family. We all thought that was the end of that.

A few years later, she began her next major creative project, building a house on the ranch where she grew up. She inherited a parcel of land at a point overlooking Longridge Road which has been called "King's Point" for at least a hundred years. My mother said the point was named for James King, one of the first, if not the first, residents of the remote area. (He never actually owned the point, but it was just beyond his property.) The house my mother built on King's Point is a modern-day version of the Crane Place, a Victorian ranch house where she was raised.

If I walk out onto the porch from the room in my mother's house where I sit writing, I can look up the hill and see the last remnants of the Crane Place, where my grandparents raised their large family. Farther up the hill stands the house my mother's brother Frank built. If I gaze across the ridge, I can see where my uncle Adolph, my mother's other brother, has lived for the last fifty-six years. If I then look directly down into the gully beneath us, I can see where my mother's uncle Louis lived. On the other side of the house, I can look out over the South 20, where my mother's uncle Otto lived.

As far as I know, I am unique amongst my friends in this regard. They all think it's terribly Old World to have one's past and present relations clustered in nearby hills and dales.

But this was the vision my mother had. Others might wince at the thought of going back to childhood in their waning years. She desired nothing less than to recreate her childhood home and memories as nearly as possible.

Unfortunately she became ill just as she was putting the finishing touches on her home. When I saw her ensconced in her version of the ranch house, frantically gathering together photographs and memorabilia for posterity, I couldn't help but think of my grandmother. I suggested we dust off the old manuscript and publish it in a more permanent form. She responded with her typical enthusiasm.

In her remaining months, she interviewed some of the old timers from the mountains, gathering new stories. She worked long hours every day on the book, even while fussing with doctors and treatments. In the end, I'm convinced her dedication to the book extended her life by several months.

Tragically, she wasn't able to see the book published. But I'm certain she had a very clear picture of it in her mind. She went over and over galleys up until a few days before her death.

She expired October 19, 1994 in her home on Longridge Road, not more than a minute's walk down hill from where her mother had died twenty years earlier in "The Last Story."

J. Alex Tarquinio
Skyland, Calif.
July 3, 1995

The Crane Place — An overview of the major structures as seen looking down from the vineyard, c. 1930s. Center: the main house. The cabin far right was the oldest building on the property. Front l. to r.: wash house, well, delco light battery, garage.

THE CRANE PLACE

MAMA LIVED IN THE SANTA CRUZ MOUNTAINS from her thirteenth birthday, in 1901, to one day before her eighty-seventh birthday. She was a born storyteller and her subjects ranged from her father's birth in an Indian village in Wisconsin territory to cometic anecdotes about the characters living up in the Santa Cruz Mountains. Mama could rouse the emotions and make you want to laugh...or cry, depending on the tale she was telling. There were some who objected to her whooping and hollering and swearing when she was conjuring up Aunt Lydia or Salvadore. Both of these individuals were loud and boisterous by nature and given to much cursing and colorful language.

Occasionally Mama would drug her audience with one of her large farm meals. Everyone would be in such a drowsy state, drifting in and out of consciousness, and in various positions of repose. Mama had a captive audience then. Sometimes when the Delco light battery had lost its charge and needed to be regenerated, or when we simply could not afford the three hundred dollars to buy a new battery, we reverted to kerosene lamps or candles. Just when Mama needed that extra touch of lighting or sound, it seemed that she would conjure up an electrical storm, with its accompaniment of thunder, lightning and heavy rain pelting down upon the galvanized tin roofing. Or could it be that she would take advantage of this timing to tell her story of the Civil War days? You could swear you heard the drum beat and the roar of the cannons as they flashed against the backdrop of the stormy night sky. Occasionally even an earthquake occurred at the right moment to punctuate one of her stories.

She lived in the house where I grew up, the Crane

Place,[1] from 1915 until her death in 1975. The house had eleven outside doors and none of them were ever locked in all of those years. When Mama was a young teenager, about fifteen, she had worked in the Crane Place for a dollar a day, helping to clean up after their drunken revelries. She never expected then that one day she would become the lady of the house!

The Crane Place had been a mansion in its day. When I was growing up, it was still an unusual setting for Mama's stories. It had an air of mystery. It had many doors leading from its larger rooms—for example, there were seven doors leading off of the ballroom, which we called the Big Room. There were two fireplaces, one in the dining room and one in the Big Room, each with carved mantels and pictorial tiles with scenes from long ago days. The walls in the big room were covered with perfect redwood paneling. Each strip was four inches wide and reached the entire twelve foot height of the walls.

High on the walls—which seemed enormous to me as a child—hung pictures of my father's parents who came over from Germany in the 1860s to settle in Missouri. Their austere portraits peered down on us from their large oval frames for sixty years. On this same wall, the head of a deer hung that had been shot and mounted by Uncle Bert, my mother's younger brother. It also hung there for sixty years. My son Ken told me this terrified him as a child, as it also terrified me when I was a small child.

Papa gave in to his one pleasurable vice in 1922. He bought a professional billiard table from a pool hall in San Jose which was going out of business. From that time until 1980, it stood on one end of the Big Room. Papa had many happy times playing billiards. Some of the neighbors thought he was going straight to hell. They already knew he was a heathen—after all he was a Catholic! Nevertheless, many of

---

[1] Properties in and around the Summit area of the Santa Cruz Mountains are still referred to by the name of the family that first owned them, thus: the Crane Place, the Blabon Place, the Hoops Place. It makes no difference if these families have been gone for a hundred years—the tradition persists. (Ed.)

The rose bush flourishes — Background: 100-year-old rose bush. Back row: Emma Ingraham Rapp (Mama), Adolph Rapp (Papa). Front row: Margaret, Frank and Mary Rapp, 1940.

the local menfolk would drop in after their chores to join Papa in a game of pool. In the summertime, the pool table was in constant use. The hired hands would have a game or two after lunch and before going back to work. The kids would play the rest of the day. We were pretty hard on it, and finally ripped the felt in two places. Papa had to pay two hundred dollars to have it refinished. After that he insisted that it was always covered when not in use, and only let his grandchildren play on it when they reached twelve. This became one of our family's rites of passage.

There were only three bedrooms in this huge house, which had been built primarily for entertaining. So my brother Adolph used the big bathroom off of the organ room with a sink and a tub for his room. (As elegant as this house had been in its day, we still had to trek outside to the outhouse. We used the Sears and Roebuck Catalogue as both reading material and toilet paper.)

The room right off of the Big Room, that was meant to be a parlor but which Mama called the Bay Window Room, functioned as a bedroom for my two oldest sisters, Elizabeth and Emma Mae. Off of this room, there was a balcony which inspired no end of imaginative play. It was used as a house when we played with dolls. Later it was used as a fort when we played Cowboys and Indians. Still later it was used for playing "Romeo and Juliet."

The main door led into the foyer, off of the ballroom. However, as you came up the long, winding driveway and parked your buggy, or in later years your truck or car, the rooms nearest you were the dining room, living room and kitchen. We usually entered through the dining room or kitchen door. The living room also had bay windows. We called this the parlor. It had two large sliding doors between the living room and dining room. We used these as curtains for our summer performances.

The kitchen alone had six doors. One led outside through the east entrance. One led into the cloak room, which went into the dining room. One led into the servant's bathroom (which was part of the maid's quarters, in the old days), and the fourth one led into the pantry. There was a pass closet leading into the dining room through which the cook was meant to pass the food to the butler, if you were fortunate enough to have servants. The sixth door went into the cooler. We didn't have a refrigerator until I was twelve years old. In the cooler, the cold air was allowed to come up from under the house through a hole in the floor. We kept our pans of milk in there after milking the cow. The butter churn also sat in there, waiting for the cream to be collected off the top of the milk pans.

The whole house sounds confusing? How do you think we felt the first five years of our lives, before we learned how to read a map? To top it off, there were porches on every side of the house. Mama had them all named. There was the East Porch, where Mama liked to sun herself in her later years. There was the Big Porch, which wrapped around the south and west sides of the house. The porch on the south side of the house was covered, and in the summertime we all brought our beds out there to camp out. Also on the west side, but off of the Bay Window Room, was the balcony where we used to play. And then there was the North Porch, which was supposed to be the main entrance, but was rarely used as such. The children not only needed a map to get around the house, we needed to know our polar directions!

THE CRANE FAMILY built this mansion in 1890 as a summer home. The family resided in San Francisco. The mother, Sarah Crane, died in 1898. She left three children: Leonard A. Crane, Catherine McAlpine Farrington, and Frank H. Crane. Her son Leonard was the executor of the will, and in 1900 he inherited the property in the Santa Cruz Mountains.

Then he and his wife Mabel squandered all their money, throwing wild parties and buying the best of everything. Champaign glasses were thrown against the fireplaces. The Fidels, who operated a winery in Skyland at the turn of the century, "despite the fact that Skyland is of a temperance order,"[2] had the Crane's listed many, many times

---

[2] To quote J.J. Bamber in his publication *The Realty*, November, 1902, Issue No. I. (Ed.)

in their books. When the money was gone, Leonard and Mabel divorced and sold their property on Longridge Road to the Rapp brothers, who purchased it on February 5, 1906. The three Rapp brothers made a down payment of ten dollars in gold coins of the United States of America. This left them with a mortgage of $2,500, for forty acres and the Crane's palatial mansion.[3]

When their marriage was new, Leonard and Mable Crane planted a sprawling white rosebush on the south side of the house, right next to the Big Porch. In 1933, Mr. and Mrs. Crane both came back to see it. They came separately, and without each other's knowledge. The old rosebush is still there, a hundred years later.

The house was perched on top of a high hill, on forty acres, with a magnificent view of the entire Monterey Bay and the Pacific Ocean on the south, a huge stand of redwood trees on the north, another hill with a vineyard to the east, and a lovely view on the west with the most equisite sunsets you can imagine.

There was a small cellar under the house where canned foods and bottled beverages were kept. There was also a large cavernous space under the rest of the house. Some of the older children played there. I was never that brave. At Mama and Papa's fiftieth wedding anniversary, Clara confessed that that was where she had hidden whenever she had done something naughty. If she and my older brother

---

[3] The history of the Crane's property in Skyland is interesting. When Leonard and Mabel sold their property to the Rapp's in 1906, the Crane family had owned it for twenty-four years. They were not very far removed from when the parcel was a small part of the historic Spanish Ranch. Leonard's mother Sarah was given the property ten years before her death, on May 15, 1888, by Charles W. Crane. He gave it to her, "In consideration of his love for her, and so that she may be better able to maintain herself..." He was presumably her husband. In 1888, the parcel Charles gave her was 320 acres, eight times the size of the property the Crane's had left by 1906.

Charles Crane had bought this parcel on June 5, 1882 from Mary Flatt, for $2,500. She had bought the 320 acre parcel in 1878 from L. Ries. The Ries family had purchased it on May 14, 1875 from a land company. The parcel was listed on the deed as part of the Rancho San Vincente. (cont'd.)

Relaxing with a game of billiards — l. to r.: Brother as a child, Henry Garner, Mama, Papa (at play).

had gotten into trouble together, Brother would get his spanking as he was a year younger and couldn't get away quickly. Then Mama would call, "Clara! Clara!" She would hear Clara's little voice answering very softly, "Yes, Mama!" But Mama could never tell where the voice was coming from.

During the winters, most of the house was cold. The two fireplaces never drew smoke well after the bricks all came tumbling down in the 1906 earthquake. The only other heat came from a wood burning stove in the kitchen and a pot bellied stove in the living room.

I much preferred summers. The house was very comfortable then, as the tall ceilings and the huge attic with lots of air space was like an insulator and the house was comfortably cool. When I was little, the house seemed dark, creaky and frightening in the winter. In the summer, it came to life when my older brothers and sisters came home from school for their three months vacation, and my cousins came from the city of Stockton. Since it was hot in Stockton, and since Aunt Belle and Uncle Ernest liked to travel, they would leave Phyllis to play with my sister Mary, and Janet to play with me. Virginia would stay at Aunt Ida's house for the summer as she was nearer to my cousin Barbara's age. Aunt Ida lived about three and a half miles from us on the north side of the hill from Skyland.

Every summer when I was growing up in the 1930s, we all got together and performed summer theater for our neighbors. We would crank out all of the numbers on our party telephone line. We invited everyone from miles around.

(cont'd from previous page)

The American settlers dubbed this ranch the "Spanish Ranch" because it was created by a Mexican land grant. On June 11, 1841, Pio Pico, then constitutional governor of California, granted the land to Blas Escamillia. In 1853, Escamillia petitioned the U.S. government to recognize his claim to the land, under the 1851 Congressional Act to Ascertain and Settle Private Land Claims in the State of California. His peitition was confirmed on January 23, 1855, although it was not sealed by President Grant, filed and recorded until 1870. (Ed.)

Mama had many busy summers. Besides a house full of children and cousins, she had an ailing husband to care for, the farm to run, and the hired hands to feed and house. They usually stayed in the cabins and outer buildings. Salvadore was frequently there excavating (his word for digging.) And this was during the depression!

During these busy years, Mama did most of her storytelling in the winter months, when we would sit in front of the fire and shell walnuts.

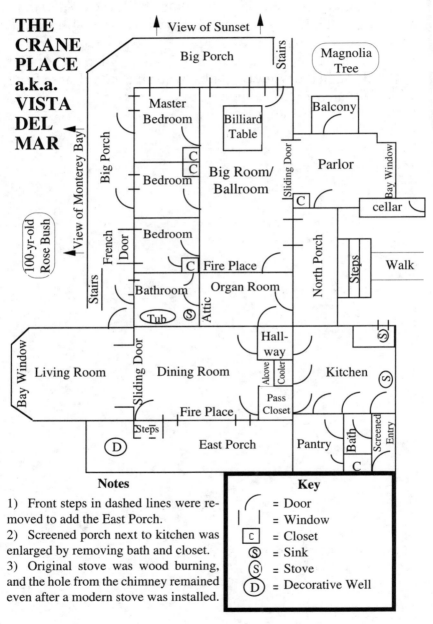

THE CRANE PLACE a.k.a. VISTA DEL MAR

View of Sunset

Big Porch

Stairs

Magnolia Tree

Master Bedroom

Billiard Table

Balcony

Big Porch

View of Monterey Bay

C
C

Bedroom

Big Room/ Ballroom

Sliding Door

Parlor

Bay Window

C

cellar

100-yr-old Rose Bush

French Door

Bedroom

C   Fire Place

Organ Room

North Porch

Steps

Walk

Stairs

Bathroom

Attic

Tub   Ⓢ

Hall-way

Ⓢ

Bay Window

Living Room

Sliding Door

Dining Room

Alcove   Cooler

Kitchen

Ⓢ

Ⓢ

Pass Closet

Fire Place

Steps

D

East Porch

Pantry   Bath   Screened Entry

C

Notes

1) Front steps in dashed lines were re-moved to add the East Porch.

2) Screened porch next to kitchen was enlarged by removing bath and closet.

3) Original stove was wood burning, and the hole from the chimney remained even after a modern stove was installed.

Key

⌒ = Door

| | = Window

[c] = Closet

Ⓢ = Sink

Ⓢ = Stove

Ⓓ = Decorative Well

Based on a sketch by Emma Mae Lydon

DESTINATION: WRIGHT'S

A BOUT FIFTY YEARS BEFORE Mama moved to the Santa Cruz Mountains, Charley McKiernan, better known as Mountain Charley, expanded on the Zayante Indian trails, with the help of some of his friends. The Zayantes lived in the Santa Cruz Mountains as recently as the 1840s; but their way of life ended soon after the first American settlers arrived. Rugged characters like Mountain Charlie occupied that space, which existed for a brief period of time, between the old Santa Cruz Mountains of the Zayantes and the new settlements which sprang up in the 1870s and '80s, such as Skyland, Burrell, Laurel and Wright's.[4]

In the second half of the last century, Mountain Charley and his friends charged stage coaches and others a toll to travel across the roads they had expanded upon in the 1850s. This was not always appreciated. Once a circus wanted to travel across the mountains to Santa Cruz. Mountain Charley was going to charge the circus for each animal. The man said that he would just let the lions out of their cages. Mountain Charley countered by saying, "I have a bullet for every one of your lions." The man paid Mountain Charley his toll.

In those days, there were lots of deer, coyotes, mountain lions and cougars in the Santa Cruz Mountains—all of which can still be seen there today, except in smaller num-

---

[4] From the very beginning, this train station, postal stop and boom town had two alternate spellings of its name: one with and one without the possessive apostrophe. For simplicity, we standardize the spelling in this book and use "Wright's" unless we are quoting a letter in which the original author did not use the apostrophe. (Ed.)

bers.[5]

There were also plenty of grizzly bears. Mountain Charley became famous in 1854 for a fight he had with a grizzly. Mountain Charley was a crack shot, but this time he only wounded the bear. He tried to stab it with his knife but he lost it. Then he had to fight the wounded bear with his bare hands. He got a hole in his head and one of his eyes was put out, but he killed the grizzly.

MOUNTAIN CHARLEY McKIERNAN is not to be confused with Silent Charley Parkhurst, one of the stagecoach drivers of that time and another notable character. From 1868 on, Silent Charley was one of the most famous drivers on the old San Jose-Santa Cruz stage coach run. A tough looking character, Charley had once been kicked in the face by a horse, losing an eye. He wore an eye patch over the eye socket. Curiously, he went unshaven, which was unusual for the tough-minded whips of that time. It wasn't until the death of Charlie Parkhurst in 1879, that it was discovered that "he" had been a "she," and had been christened Charlotte Parkhurst.

Charlotte had learned her trade as a youth in Vermont, where she began her masquerade as a man. She drove a stage coach run in Utah for a while, until the Mormons started querying "Charley" why he didn't take a couple of wives. That's what drove Charley out west, to the Santa Cruz Mountains.

Charley Parkhurst may have been the first woman to vote in the United States. Of course, she voted under the guise of a man.

Charley raised cattle in her later years. Upon her death, her partner, Woodard, another "bachelor" wrangler, was quite upset to learn of the deception she had practiced on him for so many years.

THE FIRST AMERICAN SETTLERS came to the Santa Cruz Moun-

---

[5] Los Gatos, the last town in Santa Clara Valley before you reach the Santa Cruz Mountains, was named for the wild cats roaming these hills. (Au.)

It was the fastest and nosiest mule team in the mountains! Earl Hanaford, the first mailman in the Santa Cruz Mountains, delivering mail to the residents serviced from Wright's post office, 1918.

tains in the 1850s and 1860s. Although many of these families have either died out or left the area, many of their names still live on in the form of place names in the Summit area.

The Schultheis family built the first home in the Santa Cruz Mountains, near where Summit Road is now, in 1852. Their neighbors, the Averill family, made their way to the Santa Cruz Mountains in the wake of the American Civil War. The Chase family arrived in the 1860s and established a saw mill.

The Burrells and the Wrights had intermarried before they moved to the Santa Cruz Mountains. They first moved to the mountains in 1853, and began homesteading. More of their relations followed from back east. The Wright's name became famous as a place name for the prominent train station, pleasure spot, and boom town which had its heyday from 1880 until the early part of this century. The Burrell's leant their name to another, smaller community around the Summit area. The little community of Burrell would become the future site of the center for telecommunications in the mountains during the early part of the next century.

The Burrells married into the Morrell family, and thus began another prominent early mountain family. The Morrell family, which still has a road named after it off of Summit Road, settled into the Summit area in 1867. They planted vineyards, and eventually ventured into the lumber business.

A RAILROAD WAS COMPLETED IN 1880, connecting the Santa Clara Valley with Santa Cruz. Service to the main train station in the Santa Cruz Mountains, Wright's, officially commenced on May 15, 1880. During construction, Wright's was a temporary home and way-station for the gangs of (principally Chinese) laborers on the railroad. The place also attracted those in search of one of the few spots where you could still live in the "Wild West." It was famous for its lawlessness and saloons.

Then came the boom town years. Wright's station became an important shipping point for the agricultural and lumber industries. Hotels sprang up to entertain the flocks of

Wright's Railroad Station — This was probably taken around the time that service commenced in 1880.

summer tourists. There were parks, and picnic groves, and pleasant walks.

Another lure to tourists was the famous Wright's Rifle Club, where world class marksmen gathered to test their skill. This flourished from 1905 to 1915, when World War I sadly depleted the ranks of its membership. The club was founded by John Utshcig, who was also president of the Austro-German colony at Austrian Gulch.

With the opening of the railroad came the population explosion! Tourists rushed from San Francisco in droves, particularly in the summertime. Because of their tremendous natural beauty, the Santa Cruz Mountains was a favorite stopping place for many of the weary travellers. A tourism industry sprang up to accomodate them.

The Miltonmont, a fancy hotel, was built by Judge George Miller in the 1880s to house his friends who came up from the Santa Clara Valley, where he resided. It was located in Skyland, at the intersection of Miller Hill and Miller Cut Off.[6]

This is the real life Judge Miller who is depicted at the beginning of Jack London's novel *Call of the Wild*. Jack London also spent time in the Santa Cruz Mountains; and, in fact, there is a road near Holy City named "Call of the Wild Road."

The Willows, at the junction where Skyland, Stetson, and Longridge roads meet, was the most well known resort in the mountains at the end of the last century. It is only about one mile from the Crane Place. The Willows was a much larger property then than it is now.[7]

Donald Beadel purchased the property for The Willows from the mountains' largest land and lumber lord, Frederic A. Hihn. Originally from Germany, legend has it that Hihn landed in the Santa Cruz Mountains with nothing

[6] After Judge Miller's death in the 1920s, his son Anson operated Miltonmont as a resort hotel. It has a spectacular view of the Pacific Ocean. For several years during the 1950s, it was a private mental hospital. Today it is a private residence. (Au.)
[7] The Willows is still in operation, although currently it functions as a residential trailer park. (Ed.)

but a pack on his back. He proceeded to buy up much of the local property. By the time Beadel purchased the site for The Willows from him, in 1886, Hihn owned thousands of acres, and employed many of the local residents in his lumber operations.

Beadel's son Alex made many improvements to The Willows early in this century, including building an indoor swimming pool which was the largest in the United States at that time. Newspapers as far off as the east coast featured the indoor swimming pool and its exotic setting.[8]

THE LUMBER INDUSTRY was a major part of the early economy in the Santa Cruz Mountains, particularly after the railroad was built and it became easier to transport the lumber down into the towns. There were several big saw mills in the mountains, buzzing and humming from sun up to sun down.

Although the Hihn family was without a doubt the largest lumber concern in the mountains, several of the other prominent early settlers also made their fortunes in the lumber business. Many of them had come seeking gold, but soon discovered that it was in the trees.

The Chase family owned one of the first lumber mills on Summit Road. The Young family was also a pioneer in the early lumber industry, operating a mill at what became Wright's, and also one at the intersection of Hall and Summit Roads. Mrs. Comstock owned a vast lumber mill near Hester Creek, which extended to the Willows. Mountain Charlie, who was still around in the 1880s, had a saw mill for a short time right after the railroad started running. There was a mill near Laurel at the same time. It was owned by the Morrell family. There was also a box and crate mill at Skyland. It

---

[8] I remember the lovely English-style home where my mother's best friend, Mrs. Parker, lived in the 1920s. There were also many cabins. It still had the large indoor swimming pool which we all used. It had been a resort before the Parkers purchased it in the 1920s, but they didn't operate it as such. They sold the public part of it in 1934 to the Enloes, who began renting out the cabins to tourists again. The Parkers kept a small parcel of the land for themselves, and built a cottage. (Au.)

Working at the sawmill — Foreground: Hiram Ingraham at his sawmill in the redwood grove on the Crane Place.

supplied the fruit farmers with crates.

There were many more redwoods in the Santa Cruz Mountains in the first part of the century. Besides the thriving lumber industry, a lot of land was cleared to make room for the farmers to plant orchards and vineyards.

FRUIT WAS FAST BECOMING a big cash crop. Prunes, pears, grapes, apricots, apples, plums, and cherries were sold in large quantities in San Francisco, particularly the grapes. Once the railroad started running, it was about as easy to ship produce all the way to San Francisco as it was to truck it down into the valley. There were canneries in San Jose which canned some of the pears and dehydrated the prunes.

Because of the higher altitude, the Santa Cruz Mountains had more rain than the valley. There wasn't any need to irrigate the orchards and the vineyards. It wouldn't have been possible anyway, because of the steep hills. Irrigation makes the fruit larger, but not as sweet. The fruit swells up with more water and less sugar. The farmers in the valley irrigated their crops so that they would fetch a better price. But the fruit in the Santa Cruz Mountains was famous for being so sweet.

Along with the vineyards, small wineries began cropping up. The main one in Skyland in the early part of this century belonged to our neighbors, the Fidels. Marcus Fidel came over from Switzerland in the early 1880s. He purchased the property next to the Crane Place shortly thereafter.

He met his wife, Emma, in Soquel. She was a young woman from Detroit, who had always wanted to go to California. She had just arrived on the train when she met Marcus. They married in 1885. He built a small house, even though there was already an older building on their property. They had four chidren: Arno, Marie, Steffi, and Eloise. They operated a winery in Skyland; and as far as I can tell, they never had any troubles with this during prohibition.

But the heyday of the Santa Cruz Mountains was short lived. The vineyards were severely cut back in the early 1900s due to an agricultural disease, although some did remain through the 1930s.[9] Most of the agricultural industry died out in the early 1930s, due to the hardships of the depression. Then fruit farming in the mountains was severely cut back again in the 1940s and 1950s. After the railroad stopped running in 1938, it was much more difficult for the farmers to get their produce to market.

The farmers in the valley just had too many economic advantages over those in the mountains. They had level ground and they were closer to the market. Also, once so many of the redwoods in the mountains had been chopped down, the soil began to erode and it wasn't as fertile as it had once been.

---

[9] Today there is something of a resurgence of vineyards in the Santa Cruz Mountains, as many Californian wineries are once again discovering how sweet grapes grown in this region are. (Ed.)

GO WEST YOUNG MAN

MAMA ALWAYS LOVED the American Indians, even before it was fashionable to do so. When I was a little girl, she would tell me stories about them. Not many years before, she told me, they had roamed the very hills where we lived. The roads we travelled on had been their trails. These stories fascinated me.

Mama told me about her ancestors from the east, and their travels across the frontier. According to Mama, her own father, Hiram, had been born in an Indian village. She said the local Indians helped deliver her father when her grandmother gave birth on their way through the territories in 1854.

Joseph Ingraham married Caroline Smith.[10] Then they left Connecticut and started walking west with just the barest of essentials: a frying pan, a blanket, a little food and the clothes on their backs. They wanted to stake their land claim in the "Great Western Frontier," which was in Iowa at that time. They were full of high spirits, high hopes, and in good health. Caroline was fifteen and Joseph was twenty-four.

After many miles, their footsteps began to lag. Caroline was pregnant. She went into labor one night on the trail. Joseph built a large fire to protect her from the animals. Indians spotted the fire. The women helped Caroline with her delivery. Then she stayed with them while her husband went on and built their log cabin, and came back for her and little Hiram.

In a few years, they had two more sons, Fred and James, and their daughter, Lizzie.

---

10 Hiram always said she was related to Captain John Smith. (Au.)

JOSEPH JOINED THE NORTHERN ARMY when the Civil War broke out. He left his young family to care for themselves. He joined up September 10, 1861. Just three months later, December 3, 1861, he died of typhoid fever.

Caroline had an impossible time fending for herself and her four young children. She resorted to stealing pickets from neighboring fences to try to keep her family warm. She was only twenty-nine when she died of extreme hardship, exposure to the cold winter, starvation, and eventually tuberculosis.

Mama said when her father got to this part of his story, he would always get out his handkerchief, shed a few tears and blow his nose, before going on to tell of his experiences in the orphanage.

Hiram was still very young when he was orphaned, and his three younger brothers and sisters were with him for a short time. Then he was caught stealing potatoes from the pantry. The orphans were given very little to eat, so Hiram and some of the older boys stole potatoes and, after everyone had gone to bed, they would go out into the fields and roast them over hot coals. When he was caught, Hiram was severely beaten. He ran away, but not before making a pact with his younger siblings to meet at a specified time and place in the future.

After running away, Grandpa lived with a Baptist minister in Iowa. When he got older, he started doing odd jobs on the local farms. He got a job working for Grandma Susan's father, and that's how the young couple met.

Hiram and his brother Fred never did keep in touch too well. Fred died, and we never did learn much about him. His brother James married and had a second hand store in Gridley, California. He and his wife had two daughters.

Lizzie married Grandma Susan's brother Jasper. They continued living in Iowa for a short time. Jasper died only a few years after their marriage. He was digging a well and it caved in on him. They had one daughter, Lydia.

Lizzie wound up in Scott City, Kansas. She made several trips out west to visit her brother Hiram. The last of these was on the occasion of Hiram and Susan's fiftieth wedding anniversary, in October of 1926. By this time, Hiram and Susan had had a falling out with Lizzie, and she was an unwelcome guest.

THE INGRAHAM FAMILY

SUSAN JEWELL was a very frail child. She had a weak heart and was thought to be dying when she was four years old. The neighbors all gathered around her bed, mourning and grieving. They said, "Oh, the poor little tyke, she's not gonna make it. She's a goner for sure." Susan couldn't speak as she lay there partially conscious, but she could hear them. And from that day forward, she was always very careful about what she said and how she acted around sick people. She would say to Mama, "You know, Emmy, sick people might look like they don't know what's going on, but they can hear you. And it can be very frightening for them—especially for young children."

Susan always had a very sweet nature and an even temper. This was exemplified in the episode of the blue willow platter. This platter has been in our family over one hundred and fifty years, originally belonging to Susan's mother Alvina Jane, in Kentucky. In fact, the set of blue willow dishes was one of the few possessions the Jewell family took with them in the covered wagon whenever they moved from one part of the country to another.

Susan's older sister Ellen was a high strung girl, often acting impulsively and impetuously. One day she took the dish pan with the platter still in it and threw the entire contents into the yard. Their mother was so exasperated with Ellen for throwing the platter out with the dishwater she said, "As the eldest daughter, you were to receive my blue willow dishes. But you were so careless with the platter, that the dishes will go to Susan. She will take better care of them." The platter has a small chip in the back of one of the corners as evidence of that event.

Susan did get the set of dishes. Upon her death in

38

1927, her oldest living daughter, Emma (Mama), inherited the platter. The rest of the dishes had broken during the 1906 earthquake. The platter went to my oldest sister, Elizabeth, in 1975. Her oldest granddaughter, Karen, received it in 1994.

When I was growing up, we only used the platter on very special occasions, usually Thanksgiving and Christmas turkey dinners. Mama would always advise us to handle it carefully—especially while doing the dishes. That's usually when she told us the story of the platter and how privileged she was to have it.

SUSAN'S MOTHER was married twice. Her maiden name was Alvina Jane Kitt. She and her first husband, Mr. Scott, had five children before she was widowed. One night Mr. Scott heard the cry "horse thief!" In those days, when someone cried "horse thief!" every able bodied man would jump on his horse and try to catch the culprit. Unfortunately Mr. Scott must not have had his full wits about him after being woken up by the cry of alarm. He smacked his horse on the rump to wake it up. The horse kicked him in the head, and he died instantly.

Alvina Jane Kitt Scott later married Susan's father, Preston Jewell, who was a Texas Ranger. She bore six more children. This made eleven children in all that she gave birth to. Preston, a widower, also had five boys by his previous wife. So altogether Alvina Jane raised sixteen children. This proved to be an unbearable strain on her heart, and she was bedridden for several years before her death. She was only forty-seven when she died. Susan was only sixteen.

Susan faithfully cared for her invalid mother. She fed, bathed and dressed her, and had to adjust her mother's position frequently to lessen the effect of her terrible bed-sores. After her mother died, Susan was the only one who would lay her out for burial. The neighbors all said, "Ain't it an awful thing for a young girl to have to do?" Grandma Susan replied, "My mother never hurt me when she was alive, she certainly ain't gonna now."

Later that year, October 5, 1876, Susan Elizabeth Juel

(through some quirk the spelling of her surname had changed) married Hiram Ingraham. They were married at the home of H. B. French, justice of the peace for Jackson County, Iowa. Susan was sixteen and Hiram was twenty-two.

Life was harsh for Grandma. Over the next twenty-three years she bore thirteen children. The birth dates were carefully recorded in the family Bible. Joseph was born September 25, 1877. Alvina was born June 25, 1879. Alta Mary was born December 19, 1880. Sammy was born December 26, 1881. Edgar was born November 3, 1882. George was born December 31, 1883. Francis Perry was born September 1, 1885. Clara was born February 7, 1887. Emma (Mama) was born August 9, 1888. (Mama was the ninth child, but only the third child to survive infancy and early childhood.) After Mama came Amy Ethel, who was born on August 5, 1890. Hiram Delbert (Bert), Jr. was born February 16, 1893 in Oregon. Ida Pearl was born November 10, 1900 in San Jose, California.

Alvina, George, Emma (Mama), Bert, Belle, and Ida were the only ones to survive into adulthood. The other seven children all succumbed to various illnesses and accidents, including: scarlet fever, diphtheria, fire, and drowning. Two burned in a cabin in the woods which caught fire while Grandma was fetching water from the spring. One drowned after falling into a five gallon pickle crock. And one child died in infancy with a high fever and convulsions, the cause of which was never diagnosed. This was in an isolated part of Oregon in 1890, and there was no doctor close by.

But despite these travails, Mama said her mother never carried on or screamed when she was frustrated. If she was upset, she would sit quietly and rock. The faster she rocked, the more upset the family knew she was. At last, when her rocking finally slowed and then ceased, everyone knew she was herself again.

MAMA WAS BORN in a sod hut in Kansas in 1888. Sod houses were made of wet dirt and straw, which was then formed into

Ellen Jewell, Susan's older sister. She didn't get the blue willow dishes, due to her temper.

blocks and put out to bake dry in the sun.[11]

About the time Mama was born, Alvina received a letter from her uncle in Iowa. It was from Francis Perry Juel, Susan's brother.[12]

Dear niece,

your report of the crops and times are just about as they be hear 2 years ago. Cattle sold for ten dollars a head on account of the drought and there haven't been much money in the country since. I have got two secretaries in the house now that I made last winter and can't find sale for them. Nobody seams to have eny money.

I wish you had one of them if you haven't got anything of the kind. I sometimes wish I could sell out and get where I could keep a cow and pigs. Now I only have some chickens. They are worth from $1 to $2 apiece. I sold a rooster for $1.

Well Vina, as you sead you had never written to me before, and I must excuse you, you forget that I recieved a letter from you a long time back and have got it yet. I suppose your ma has told you all about your uncle so if you should meet me, you would feel acquainted. I would like to have you come and see me and my little Clarence and Ethel and you could go to one of the nicest schools in Iowa. I live rite across the road from it and it has the nicest playground you ever saw. I got little brown legorn chickens. They look like ground squirrels or chipmunks.

Now Vina, I want you to write to me once ever month for your mama and poppy don't once a year.

Lizzie has gone to church. Both babys is a sleepe. I am alone.

Your uncle FP Juel

---

[11] There were still a few hundred-year-old sod huts standing during a road trip I made through Kansas in the 1950s. (Au.)

[12] As with all of the old letters reproduced in this book, the original errors in spelling and punctuation have been kept. Most of the people referred to here had very little formal education, and the errors have been maintained to preserve the documents' historical accuracy. (Ed.)

Alvina was nine and George was five at the time Mama was born. Because six of her mother's children had already died at an early age, Mama (by her own admittance) was a spoiled child. She was a sickly girl, and with her blonde curly hair and blue eyes, she must have resembled a fragile little doll. Her mother pampered and petted her a lot.

THE INGRAHAM FAMILY moved to Oregon in 1890. They lived in Astoria and then moved to Woodburn. Grandpa was a woodcutter. He loved the outdoors.

Mama said she could only remember one time that her mother raised her voice to Grandpa. It was one day when there was several feet of snow on the ground and Grandpa was aggravated with being cooped up in the cabin with a squalling child. He grabbed Mama, who was then three, and threw her out into the snow. Mama said she remembered all of the whiteness as she sank down into it. In her bewilderment, she stopped crying. Her father said, "That will cool her off!" That's when she heard her mother scream, "Hiram, you run out and get Emmy, now!" (Mama always said at this point in her story, "I deserved it.") Grandpa quickly rescued her and spent the rest of the afternoon rocking her, and they played with the jumping jacks that he had carved out of wood for her. These were little wooden dolls with movable arms and legs, and they jumped about as strings were pulled.

Mama saw her first orange in Oregon. In fact, she got it in her Christmas stocking. That was all she received for Christmas that year. Later, when Mama had her own family, she always made sure we always had plenty of presents under the Christmas tree. That's why I felt like crying whenever Mama told the story of her Christmas orange. Then she would tell me, "Don't feel bad, sugarplum. I was thrilled when I saw that orange. It was the first one I had ever seen and I thought it was so pretty. I almost didn't want to eat it."

Mama and her family moved to the Santa Clara Valley, in California, when she was nine years old. First they

Hiram and Susan Ingraham, with their young family, c. 1890. At back: Alvina Jane (daughter). Front l. to r.: Their children George, Emma and Ethel, who died shortly thereafter.

lived in a tent. Then they moved to a one room cabin on Doyle Road, in Cupertino. Grandpa worked on a fruit ranch. Mama told me many times about that cabin. It had a knot hole in the middle of the floor which they would sweep the dirt into, before laying the braided rug back down—a true version of sweeping the dirt under the rug.

I drove Mama to Doyle Road one day when I was about thirty, and living in San Jose. We were surprised to discover the cabin was still there. Even more amazing, the knot hole was still there! Just a few weeks later, I drove back to show my husband and children the cabin with the knot hole in the center of the floor, but it had been torn down.

MRS. SARAH WINCHESTER was a favorite topic of conversation for Mama. When Mama was eleven, her family moved from the cabin on Doyle Road to a farm house in San Jose, right across the road from Mrs. Winchester's house.[13] Mama told me she used to see Mrs. Winchester going out for a ride in her little buggy. She said Mrs. Winchester was a tiny woman— less than five feet tall. Mama also heard the hammers pounding and could see the constant building going on as the workmen went to and fro.

Mrs. Winchester inherited millions from her husband's estate. Her husband's father had invented the Winchester rifle, which claimed the lives of countless Indians. After his father's death, Mr. Winchester managed the company until his own death. The money was still pouring in from rifle sales throughout Mrs. Winchester's lifetime. In addition, the interest on her fortune alone was said to be a thousand dollars a day.

After the death of her husband and baby daughter, Mrs. Winchester consulted a psychic medium who told her she would live as long as she continued to build her house, in order to atone for the sins of her husband's family. She spared no expense in the construction of her house. She sometimes hired experts to come from Europe for a single

---

[13] This farm house was located where Town and Country Shopping Center is now. (Au.)

day's work. This was said to cost her as much as forty thousand dollars a day. She would also hire a full orchestra sometimes to come play for the dead Indian souls who she believed were haunting her mansion because they had been killed by a Winchester rifle.[14]

Although Mama had lived right across the road from Mrs. Winchester during the construction, she had never been inside the house. So years later I took Mama on the tour. She was fascinated!

ONE DAY IN 1900, Mama's family went up to the Santa Cruz Mountains to visit her sister Alvina, who had just had a baby girl named Alice. Hiram fell in love with the mountain country at first sight, which no doubt must have reminded him of the lush, green woods of Oregon, and made plans to move there as soon as possible. The family moved up to the mountains on Mama's thirteenth birthday, August 9, 1901.

Grandma Susan had been pregnant with Aunt Ida at the same time her daughter Alvina was pregnant with Alice. The two women delivered each other's babies. Alvina's came first, so Aunt Ida was already an aunt when she was born. Alvina died when she was only twenty-four, while giving birth to her second child, Ellery.

As a young girl, Alvina was sensitive and artistic. She painted dainty little pictures. And when she was a teenager in Oregon, she put flowers on all of the untended graves in the cemetery next door to where they lived. After she died, the Young family (that was Alvina's married name) moved back to Kansas where her husband George was from. This meant that Grandma Susan was separated from her two little grandchildren.

George quickly farmed the children off to relatives, and later foster homes. The little girl had an especially hard time of it. She was moved from one family to another, and was abused and molested. Finally, when Alice was fourteen,

---

[14] The Winchester Mystery House is now a local tourist attraction, and is famous for its many doors and staircases leading nowhere. (Au.)

In front of Skyland's General Store and Post Office, c. 1910s. l. to r.: Elizabeth (Lizzie) Ingraham Tyler, and proprietors Hiram and Susan Ingraham.

she was sent to live with Grandma Susan. She was a terrible burden for Grandma, as Alice was already bitter and unruly due to their bad experiences in the foster homes. She would bully Mama's young children when they went to visit Grandma.

Alice eloped with Carl Simpson, another resident of the Santa Cruz Mountains, when she was about eighteen. They had two sons, with one of them named after her brother Ellery. Later she and her husband separated, and she left the mountains for good. Alice never had anything to do with her mountain relatives after she left. She wrote Mama once and said, "The Ingraham sisters pruned me out of the family tree years ago, and I ain't a gonna be grafted back on now."

SUSAN'S CLOSEST FRIEND and confidante was Clara Leask. Her husband founded Leask's department store in downtown Santa Cruz, which was originally called the Seaside Department Store on Pacific Avenue. The Leask family used to come up to the mountains for a few weeks each summer.

The two women were kindred spirits. Both ran stores, although the Leask's were much better off than their counterparts in the mountains. Grandma was never one to spend much on herself, so each summer Mrs. Leask brought her a new dress from their store and passed it off as one from her own closet. She always said, "Samuel just hates this dress on me. Won't you please take it off my hands, Susan?"

I have a letter Clara Leask sent to my grandmother in 1926. It was in answer to an invitation for Susan and Hiram's fiftieth wedding anniversary celebration. She wrote:

Dear Friends,
Mr. Leask and I regret that it is impossible for us to present our good wishes personally, so we are taking this poorer way to congratulate you on your fiftieth anniversary.

It is a great and good thing to have lived to-gether for fifty years, rearing a large family creditably and all the while living in a way that has endeared you, not only to those in the family circle, but also to a large number of people among

All aboard! — Bert Ingraham in his conductor's uniform for the Southern Pacific Railroad.

whom you have worked and lived.
    Many more years of living and loving.
    Sincerely,
    Clara J. Leask

    Unfortunately, Grandma lived only four more months.

SUSAN'S GREATEST SORROW during her lifetime was caused by the unfortunate series of events effecting Uncle Bert, one of her few surviving children. Bert was working as a conductor on the Southern Pacific Railroad, when he fainted while jumping off the train as it was coming into a station and injured his head. He was in a coma for months, and when he finally came out of it, he was prone to epileptic seizures. He also had continuous headaches and dizzy spells. He was afraid he would never be the same again, and he became very depressed. He was only twenty-seven years old.

On January 25, 1920, Bert went into his mother's room. She was not quite awake yet. He kissed her and said, "I love you, Mama. I always will." He left her room, shutting the door softly.

The night before, Bert had stayed up late visiting with his good friend Johnny Wood, who lived at the Woolcott Place. This was about two miles away, down at the end of Longridge Road. Bert and Johnny had been classmates in grammar school, and Johnny was pleased to see that Bert seemed to be feeling a little bit more like himself again.

Johnny and his wife Florence were renting the Woolcott Place at that time, and Florence was away at the hospital giving birth to their first child, Jack. So Bert knew Johnny would be home alone as he headed back down to the Woolcott Place on that brisk winter morning.

Johnny was still in his slippers when he answered the door. Bert told him he had enjoyed their visit the night before. Johnny said, "I did, too." Then Bert said he had noticed a lot of quail down by the trees, and asked Johnny if he would loan him his shotgun so he could go shoot a few.

After Johnny gave him the gun, Bert turned it on him and said, "Now you get out of here!"

Johnny fled up to the Fidel's, stumbling and tripping over his floppy slippers. It was uphill all the way, and Johnny burst in on them trembling and out of breath. Arno, Steffi, and Eloise Fidel, who were all teenagers, were there. Arno and Steffi accompanied Johnny back down to his place to investigate.

Bert was there when they got back. It must be difficult to fatally shoot yourself with a shotgun. He had only injured himself the first time; but the second time he had delivered a fatal shot to his head. His body was lying on Johnny's porch.

When the coroner came to pick up Bert's body, he just wrapped it in a tarp and strapped it to the back of his car. All of Skyland stared in shock as the coroner's car left the mountains with its gruesome cargo. Bert had been well loved in the community, with a reputation for mildness and generosity. No one could believe he had done such a terrible thing.

Johnny Wood, and Arno and Steffi Fidel all had to attend the inquest the next day. Coroner W.R. Congdon determined the cause of death to be a "gunshot wound with suicidal intent."

The Leask family took over the details of Bert's funeral. He was buried the day after the inquest, on January 27, 1920. Following this tragedy, Susan's health and outlook on life declined rapidly, until her death six years later.

Mama never did like the Southern Pacific Railroad after this. She thought they hadn't done enough for her little brother after his accident on the job. He had no means of support, and thought he would never be employable again. Also, he must have been in some physical pain.

Her brother's death was such a painful memory for Mama that she never told me this story herself. I pieced it together from stories that Aunt Belle, Aunt Ida, my sister Elizabeth, and Eloise Fidel told me over the years. Also, the one time I met Samuel Leask, when he was ninety-seven years old, he mentioned the tragic incident. He said, "It was so sad about Bert. He was such a fine young fellow."

BERT HAD AN EASY GOING disposition, and a generous spirit. He

Bert is captured here in a winsome pose, May 4, 1913.

paid his sisters' way through school, putting Aunt Belle through nurse's training and Aunt Ida through San Jose Normal, present day San Jose State University.

Aunt Belle became a nurse and married Ernest Griner, a doctor. Shortly afterward, he went over to Europe to serve as a doctor in World War I. They had three daughters: Phyllis, Virginia and Janet. They lived in Stockton. When their daughters were teenagers, Aunt Belle and Uncle Ernest divorced. Aunt Belle never quite reconciled herself to the divorce.

After finishing San Jose Normal, Aunt Ida married Will Hurney and they moved to the Santa Cruz Mountains. Uncle Will was the mail carrier up in the mountains for thirty-three years. They lived in the mountains until the post office moved to Los Gatos in 1938. This occurred when the train stopped going through the mountains and delivering the mail to Wright's station, in February, 1938, after the tracks washed out in a heavy rain storm. The Hurney family moved to Los Gatos so Uncle Will could be closer to work. Also, the children were starting to enter high school, and there was none in the mountains. Uncle Will continued to deliver the mail to the mountains until about 1953, but now all mail came through the Los Gatos Post Office.

IN CONTRAST TO HIS BROTHER BERT, Uncle George was ornery. He loved to play Devil's advocate, taking the opposite side in any argument. People would get up and leave when they saw him coming. In 1915, Uncle George became a chiropractor and moved to Chicago. He never returned to the Santa Cruz Mountains. Every ten years or so, we would get a letter from him, causing much elation. This was followed by a big let down, as Mama would open her letter and all it usually said was something like, "Emma, how are you? I am fine. your brother, George." Or there was the text of this actual letter: "I will call you at five 30 March 23 Chicago time and that will be 330 California time. George." Mama would always sigh and toss the letter onto the kitchen table saying, "Oh, why does he even bother to write me? He never says anything." I have a longer letter that George wrote to his sister Ida in 1929.

> Dear sister,
> I was very much surprised to hear of the death of father. What was the cause of his death.
> It has been a long time since I left home but I hope to be in sunny Calif before long.
> I would like to see all of the family that is what is left of us before I die myself.
> You tell me you have three children. If so you have done your duty in this world.
> I have none as I am not married and no prospects of being married soon.
> How much do you think there will be left out of fathers estate after the bills are paid. Did he leave you anything in his will. How about the rest of them.
> Where is Alice; our niece now. Did Alice and Carl Simpson separate.
> What is the matter with Belle as I have never got a letter from her for many years. I have wrote her several letters but never got a reply to any.
> Is there a change in the mountains since I left them fourteen years ago.
> How is Emma's health now. Is she as stout as mother was.
> You spoke about having a cold winter there. Well we had a very cold winter here with business conditions quiet.
> Your Brother,
> George

Uncle George never did come back to California as he said he would in his letter. We heard of his death several years later. He was in his eighties by that time.

His picture hung on the wall in the First National Bank in Los Gatos for many years. I studied it every time I went into the bank. Uncle George was standing in a crevasse created by the 1906 earthquake. He was a good looking man. I never met him.

ONE OF MAMA'S HEARTACHES was that she never received a diploma. She completed the eighth grade, but in those days you needed to finish nine years to get your grammar school diploma. (Mama had a recurring dream all of her life that she was going up on stage to get her diploma.) This story always made me feel sad when she told it to me. Mama was always a great believer in education, and especially encouraged her daughters to go as far as they could.

The reason she never went beyond the eighth grade was that she often had to stay out of school to work in one of the family stores—the Ingraham's owned a General Store at Skyland and another one at Burrell. By 1906, Mama was in charge of the Burrell store. She was eighteen. Luckily when the big earthquake hit, it was 5:12 in the morning, and so no one was at the Burrell store, which was perched precariously over a gulch on Summit Road. The building was knocked over into the gully behind it, and all of the groceries and dry goods were lost in the rubble.

While the Burrell store was being rebuilt, Mama became the Skyland postmistress, which was operated out of my grandfather's store in Skyland. Once it was rebuilt, she went back to running the Burrell store, riding the five miles round trip to work on horseback. (I always thought this sounded very glamorous.)

Grandpa's job was hauling all the stock the five miles up the hill from Wright's train station, with the horse and buckboard. This was an all day job. Later on, he had a Model T Ford, and this simplified things a bit, except for when it conked out on the hill and he would have to stop and crank it back up, or sometimes even resort to pushing it the rest of the way. Luckily, those Fords were relatively light.

GRANDPA ALWAYS WANTED to have the latest modern inventions. He sent away for a telephone system when they first became available and installed it between his two stores. It was the first telephone system in the Santa Cruz Mountains, and it soon spread out to encompass the whole community.

Hiram also had great faith in the future of aeronautics. When the Wright brothers were first experimenting with

George Ingraham in Chicago. He never returned to California to see his family.

flight, in the early 1900s, he would tell his wife, "Susan, someday there'll be flying machines going over these mountains." She would say, "Oh no, Hiram, you know they could never get up this high." Grandpa also talked about men getting up to the moon someday. That was much too far fetched for practical Susan to comprehend.

While Mama was running the Burrell store, her mother ran the Skyland General Store. The family lived in back of the store at Skyland. Grandma's house seemed to sparkle with cleanliness. She kept it immaculate, even with the greatest of obstacles—no washer, dryer, or even running water. She had to haul all of her water up from the cistern with a bucket and heat it on the wood burning stove, which required a constant supply of wood that someone had to chop. Then Grandma had to scrub all of her laundry by hand and hang it out to dry on the line. Even so, she had snow-white bedspreads on all five of the beds. The flat irons were also heated on the wood burning stove. She had two, one would be heating up on the stove while she was using the other.

Her hands were always moving. To relax, she knitted or crocheted, working on a baby cap, scarf, blanket or sweater. There was always something bubbling on the stove or baking in the oven.

The front part of the house was the General Store. It was strategically placed across from the grammar school. The children loved to come at the end of their day and drool over the hore-hound drops and licorice sticks and admire the children's jewelry counter.

Susan entered the store from the back of the house anytime she heard the tinkling of the bell which meant she had a customer. Often times the person had come to chat with Grandma, just as much as they had come to buy groceries, or rope, or chicken feed. She was a natural social worker. She listened to everyone's problems and knew all of the Skyland gossip, but obviously people trusted her enough to know she would never breath a word of what they told her. For really serious matters, she had a special drawing room right off of the store with red plush curtains, a lace tablecloth on the little round table, and a fancy tea service. There, people felt secure enough to pour out their hearts.

Susan was also a midwife. She delivered over fifty babies in the Skyland community. Once when Johnny Wood was a little boy, he came into the store and asked if he could look inside the pickle barrel—the one where Mrs. Ingraham "got the babies that she delivered to the women."

THE TWO INGRAHAM GENERAL STORES were the hub of the Skyland and Burrell communities. Grandpa Ingraham, however, did not have the easygoing reputation that Grandma enjoyed in the community. Perhaps his years as an orphan had had an effect on his nervous system. He was high strung and became more cantankerous with age. He was known to have thrown a coffee pot at Mrs. Benninghoven when she arrived early at the Skyland General Store one morning. He didn't want any of her foolishness before breakfast.

Grandpa had a man working for him who was "depressed." He kept saying such things as, "The world would be a better place without me. I don't know what I'm doing here. I think I'll just end it all...." He kept repeating similar versions of these statements. Finally, Grandpa got fed up with all of his negativity. So he got a piece of heavy rope and put a noose at the end of it, then hung it up in his tool shed. The next time the man started in, Grandpa said, "Here, I thought I would help you out..." and showed him the noose. The man got so mad he chased Grandpa down the hill with a pitchfork!

Although Hiram liked automobiles later on, when they first came out around the turn of the century, he thought they were "a dern nuisance." People started flooding up from Santa Cruz on Sunday drives. It was no longer a two day trip by horse and buggy. Sometimes the automobiles scared the horses so badly that they jumped the fences and stampeded. The cows would panic, quit giving milk for a couple of days, and have to be searched for in the woods.

Grandpa said, "I'll fix those city slickers." He had a spring on his property with ample water so he turned it on Saturday and let it run all night. The next morning, when the

Front row, far r.: Ira Ingraham, Hiram's nephew, who was a wagoner in WWI.

Sunday drivers — Their air of confidence betrays that they don't know what's in store for them once they get to Skyland.

sightseers went driving through Skyland, they mired down up to their axles in mud. Grandpa Hiram then played the part of the country bumpkin, saying, "Wal, gee whiz, you should have a hoss." He got his retribution when he charged five dollars to pull the cars out of the mud. In this way, he earned twenty-five to thirty dollars in extra cash each Sunday.

The word soon spread that it was very treacherous to drive through Skyland on a Sunday morning.[15]

---

[15] A strikingly similar situation occurs in the Pulitzer Prize-winning 1962 William Faulkner novel *The Reivers*. This is purely coincidental, no doubt, and does not prevent the above story from being absolutely true. (Ed.)

GENEALOGICAL CHART #1
THE INGRAHAM FAMILY

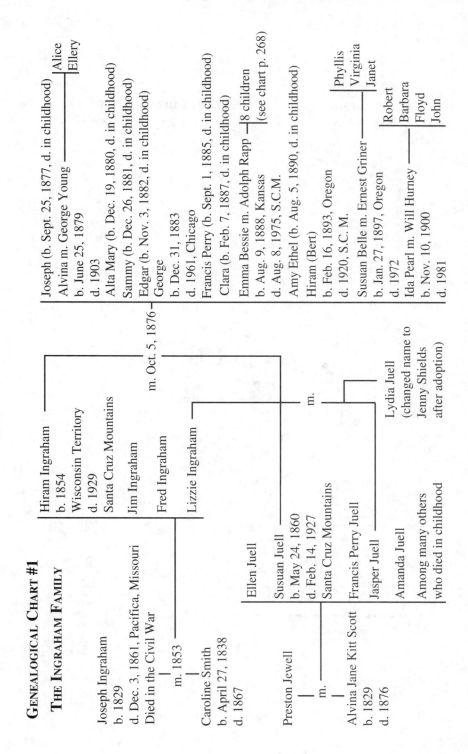

Joseph Ingraham
b. 1829
d. Dec. 3, 1861, Pacifica, Missouri
Died in the Civil War

m. 1853

Caroline Smith
b. April 27, 1838
d. 1867

Hiram Ingraham
b. 1854
Wisconsin Territory
d. 1929
Santa Cruz Mountains

Jim Ingraham

Fred Ingraham

Lizzie Ingraham

m. Oct. 5, 1876

Joseph (b. Sept. 25, 1877, d. in childhood)
Alvina m. George Young
b. June 25, 1879
d. 1903
Alta Mary (b. Dec. 19, 1880, d. in childhood)
Sammy (b. Dec. 26, 1881, d. in childhood)
Edgar (b. Nov. 3, 1882, d. in childhood)
George
b. Dec. 31, 1883
d. 1961, Chicago
Francis Perry (b. Sept. 1, 1885, d. in childhood)
Clara (b. Feb. 7, 1887, d. in childhood)
Emma Bessie m. Adolph Rapp — 8 children
b. Aug. 9, 1888, Kansas   (see chart p. 268)
d. Aug. 8, 1975, S.C.M.
Amy Ethel (b. Aug. 5, 1890, d. in childhood)
Hiram (Bert)
b. Feb. 16, 1893, Oregon
d. 1920, S.C. M.
Susuan Belle m. Ernest Griner
b. Jan. 27, 1897, Oregon
d. 1972
Ida Pearl m. Will Hurney
b. Nov. 10, 1900
d. 1981

Alice
Ellery

Phyllis
Virginia
Janet

Robert
Barbara
Floyd
John

Preston Jewell

m.

Alvina Jane Kitt Scott
b. 1829
d. 1876

Ellen Juell

Susuan Juell
b. May 24, 1860
d. Feb. 14, 1927
Santa Cruz Mountains

Francis Perry Juell

Jasper Juell

Amanda Juell

Among many others
who died in childhood

m.

Lydia Juell
(changed name to
Jenny Shields
after adoption)

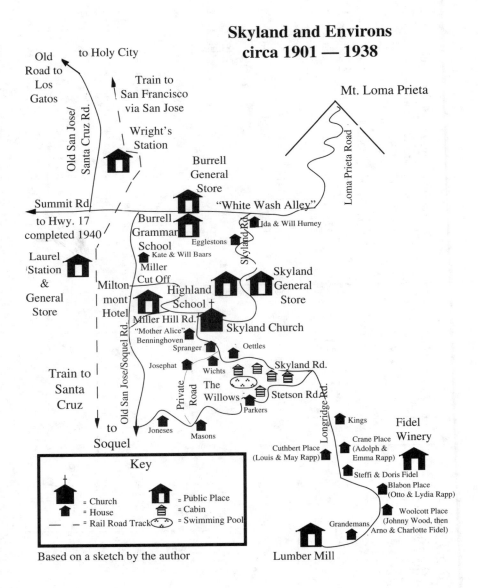

Skyland and Environs circa 1901 — 1938

Based on a sketch by the author

SKYLAND

THE SKYLAND COMMUNITY, located in the Highland district around the Summit area of the Santa Cruz Mountains, was born in the 1870s. Its name was a poetic attempt to convey the impression that this scenic spot nearly reached up to the stars. In the very first issue of *The Realty*, a news sheet written and published by local Realtor J.J. (Joseph) Bamber, he described Skyland[16] in November, 1902 thus:

"This thriving village is pleasantly situated in Highland District three miles south of Wrights on Narrow Gauge R. R. Its 2500 feet elevation gives it a commanding position. It has good mail accommodation, a separate building for a Post-office, a handsome church, a flourishing general merchandise store, pleasantly situated and well managed hotels, the Miltonmont and Hotel De Redwood. It is surrounded by many beautiful homes. The fruit and grape industry is very large while many other products are raised to profit.

"The H. F. Lawrence Box Mill furnished shingles, fruit boxes, crates, and trays and all kinds of orchard materials."

THE FIRST HIGHLAND GRAMMAR SCHOOL was built in 1883. Previously classes were held in private homes. The first

---

[16] Skyland and Highland occupied virtually the same geographic space, but they were not exactly identical. The area was first called "Highland," and primarily consisted of a few large land holdings. The Skyland settlement sprang up in the Highland district, and eventually the area became so populous that the settlement took up much of the Highland area. This led to some confusion in names. For instance, the "Highland School" was right around the corner from the "Skyland Church." (Au. & Ed.)

No. 1 | **SKYLAND, NOVEMBER, 1902**

The Realty

will be issued each month in the interest of
REAL ESTATE, FRUIT GROWING,
AND FARMING
in the Santa Cruz Mountains.

SKYLAND

This thriving village is pleasantly situated in Highland District three miles south of Wrights on Narrow Gauge R. R. Its 2500 feet elevation gives it a commanding position. It has good mail accommodation, a separate building for a Post-office, a handsome church, a flourishing general merchandise store, pleasantly situated and well managed hotels, the Miltonmont and Hotel De Redwood. It is surrounded by many beautiful homes. The fruit and grape industry is very large while many other products are raised to profit.

The H. F. Lawrence Box Mill furnished shingles, fruit boxes, crates, trays and all kinds of orchard materials.

J. J. BAMBER

REAL ESTATE AGENT

offers the following Santa Cruz Mountain and other Real Estate bargains

FOR SALE

100 ACRES of good land, situated on main County Road, 15 acres cleared. Fine Hay land. Plenty running Water. Some Timber. Price $2500. Easy terms.

10 ACRES near Skyland, on Main County Road. fine Stream running Water. Good Redwood Timber. Fertile Soil. Price $200.

25 ACRES Hay land. Some Timber. Spring and running Water. Good Soil. On splendid road. Price $900. Easy terms

30 ACRES quite level rich land. Fair New House. Grand View. Good Well and running Water. Price $1500. Easy terms.

9 ACRE Highly Improved Home, Large House, Barn, etc. All planted to best varieties of Fruits and Vines. Two good Wells of Soft Water. Drying Plant. Paying proposition. Price $1500. Half Cash.

13 ACRES Cleared Land well fenced, near Skyland. House, Barn, Chicken Houses, etc. Redwood Timber. Price $900. Small Cash Payment, balance on long time. Low interest.

25 ACRE Highly Improved Home. 13 Acres planted to best Fruits and Vines. Good House, New Barn. Plenty Water, Stock, Implements, Furniture, etc. go with place. Price $2900. Part Cash, balance on time, low interest. This is a paying property. A Bargain.

160 ACRES Choice Grape-Land above Wrights' Station. House. Part fenced and in Fruit and Vines. Only $250 to pay for improvements.

20 ACRES Paying Mineral Land at Gas Point, Shasta County, Cal., $400. For particulars, E. C. Fortier, Red Bluff, Cal.

20 ACRES near Modesto. Irrigating Water to be had. $800. Easy terms. Level and Rich Land. Make splendid home.

73 ACRES at Laurel, Santa Cruz Co. Good House, Barn, etc. Plenty good Water piped to House and Grounds. Abundance of running water. Paying Orchard. Good Timber. Fine Soil. On good road. $2500. Easy terms. A Bargain.

40 ACRES A No. 1 Redwood Land, near Wright's. Good Spring Water. Fertile Soil. On nice road. $800. Easy terms.

Splendid Villa Lot in Skyland. Good House. Grand View.

H. D. INGRAHAM

GENERAL MERCHANDISE STORE

Santa Cruz Co., Cal. **SKYLAND**

FIRE INSURANCE

P. B. WIGHTMAN

Notary Public

Post Office Building, SKYLAND, CAL.

The Realty would favor Rural Mail Delivery if our Skyland Post Office could be kept open for those wishing there Mail to come to Skyland and for the convenience of Money Orders, etc.

There is a movement on foot for a Rural Telephone Co. throughout the Bay Counties. By that means Skyland would be in communication with Soquel, Santa Cruz, Wrights and the whole neighborhood.

J. L. Wicht has built a house on lot bought through J. J. Bamber, Real Estate Agent.

Wm. G. Thornton is building on his land at Skyland, bought through J. J. Bamber, Real Estate Agent.

George Monroe is making extensive improvements on his land on Hester Creek, bought through Bamber Agency, Skyland, Cal.

J. Hummell has improved his beautiful home by an addition to his house. He also built a large fruit house.

M. Fidel has built a new Winery, improved his house and extended his Vineyard, notwithstanding Skyland is of a temperance order.

It is to be hoped the recent extensive rain fall will not destroy our late grape crops for the San Francisco Market depends on the Santa Cruz Mountains for late grapes.

It isn't the girl who fires up quickest who makes the best match.

Selfishness is a disease of which matrimony cures most people.

California was the first State in the Union to choose a State flower. In 1890 at a meeting of the State Floral Association the golden poppy was chosen.

Under the existing laws of California, no deer meat or hides can be sold.

Altitude 2225 Feet

MILTONMONT

Everything First-Class

A Home in the Santa Cruz Mountains

View of the Sea and Valley

MILTON H. MILLER. SKYLAND, CAL.

The premiere issue of J.J. (Joseph) Bamber's *The Realty*. This was the birth of a journalistic endeavor in the mountains, 1902.

school was in one room and a single teacher taught all eight grades. The older pupils helped teach the younger ones. This was a good review and, in addition, helped out the over-worked school teacher.

The original grammar school was eventually sold to the Farm Bureau, and it was used as a community hall for many years. The Skyland Library was housed at one end of the hall. My sister Emma Mae was the librarian for a while when she was in grammar school in the 1920s, earning five dollars a month.[17]

When I was in school, in the 1930s, there were four grammar schools in the Summit area: Highland (at Skyland), Burrell, Laurel and Hester Creek. Many of the local farmers found their wives from among the grammar school teachers, some of whom married less than a year after they arrived in the mountains. Caroline Hummel, Florence Wood, Ellen Lindsay, Caroline Waltz and Doris Fidel were among the women who met their husbands in this fashion.

Without a doubt, the teacher who lasted the longest at the Highland school was Eleanor Eggleston. She taught there for sixteen years. My brother Frank and I both studied with her for all eight years of grammar school. Mrs. Eggleston was famous for her double-edged compliments like, "You have such a beautiful smile, Margaret. You're brushing your teeth now, aren't you dear?" Another typical compliment was, "Your hair looks so nice now. You're combing it, and Mary is teaching you how to fix it, isn't she?"

In 1950, the four grammar schools were centralized and renamed Loma Prieta. A grammar school and middle school were built right across from each other on Summit Road. These are operated more like schools in town. The grammar school is for kindergarten through fifth grades, and the middle school is from the sixth through the eighth grades. Of course now there are different teachers for the different grade levels. My brother Adolph was chairman of the school board and a driving force behind the change. He had four

---

[17] Today the hall is a private residence. (Au.)

school age children at the time.[18]

SKYLAND CHURCH opened its doors in 1891. Before that, church services were held in the old grammar school. The new church was a lovely white building in the woods, at the intersection of Skyland Road and Miller Road. From the beginning, services were conducted in the Presbyterian faith.

The church bell was donated by Helen McEwen in 1904. She was from the east, and had seen the Skyland Church on a visit she made to the Santa Cruz Mountains. She was a friend of our neighbor on Longridge Road, James King. She had the bell shipped and, when it arrived, there was freight due. Mr. King paid it, although he was neither a member of the church, nor particularly known for his generosity otherwise.

The church was just ten years old when the Ingraham family moved to the mountains and began attending services there. Mama played the piano for Sunday services.

Later, the Skyland Church disbanded for several years. Mama was given the silver communion service, as she was the oldest member. Occasionally the church had a visiting minister, and Mama lent them the communion service. When the church hired a pastor and began weekly services again, Mama returned the communion service.[19]

THE INGRAHAM GENERAL STORE opened in Skyland in 1901. It was across the road from the old grammar school.

Hiram was always handy with inventions. In 1914, he moved the old grammar school across the yard so that they could build a new one. To do this, he constructed a pulley and wheel and powered it all with one horse power—Dolly. Aunt Ida described it like this: "One of the big deals of the neighborhood was when Papa moved the old schoolhouse to

---

[18] The school was condemned after the Oct. 17, 1989 Loma Prieta earthquake, and had to have extensive improvements. (Au.)

[19] The church was badly damaged in the 1989 earthquake. However, it has since been restored. Skyland Church celebrated its centennial in 1987, (cont'd. page 71)

Highland Grammar School, class of 1903. (cont'd. following page)

Ringing in the new century — The Skyland Church gets its bell, 1904.

Photo previous page: Highland Grammar School, class of 1903. — See how much enrollment grew in just one year! (Compare it with the photo on title page from 1902.) George Ingraham (back row, third from l.) looks older than the other students because he was. He had to work, and only returned to grammar school when he had time for a little learning. He was twenty in this picture.

   Back row l. to r.: Watson boy, Joe Hobson, George Ingraham, Madeline Watson, Miss Fickes (the teacher), Mabel Bassett, Esther Jones, Emma Ingraham and Mildred Jones. Second row: Arnold Thornton, Varlin Hummell, Watson boy, Belle Ingraham, Annie Wicht, Lucas boy, Hazel Thornton, Amere Lucas, Lucius Hobson and Louis Wicht. Front row, l. to r.: Tom Cox, Walter Wicht and Carl Hummel.

Highland Hall — The original school house, Grandpa Hiram moved this in 1914 with one horse!

its present position where it was used for many years as a hall. There was much tribulation in the neighborhood when they found out he was doing it with only one horse. He took some men into the woods and cut several trees about one foot at the base. They were skinned and put under the building. He had some heavy rope and used the horse to walk around a post. With pulleys, rope and head work, the building not only was moved about fifty feet, but it faced east instead of south. My brother (Aunt Ida's brother George) stood by the horse at all times."[20] Hiram was paid three hundred dollars for this remarkable feat.

The changes which affected the rest of the Highland community also touched the lovely Skyland. The decline in the lumber industry, agricultural production, and tourism all

(cont'd. from page 68)
and still has services, although now it is the United Church of Christ, which is its own denomination. There are now several newer churches in the mountains representing other denominations. (Ed.)
[20] My brother Frank says it was more like a hundred and fifty feet that the hall was moved. (Au.)

took their toll. Skyland is now like a ghost town. The school burned down. The Skyland General Store is no longer there. The mill is gone. The only thing that is a reminder of the past is the Skyland Church.

THE VON RAPP FAMILY

IN **1866**, Augustine von Rapp came to Illinois with his brother-in-law Martin Bertsch. They were scouting ahead to find a suitable place for the two families to immigrate to. The following year, Augustine's wife Martina came with their two daughters, Anna and Katherine, and Martina's sister-in-law, Helen Bertsch. (Augustine's niece Helen had married Martina's brother.) On the boat over, Martina's four-year-old daughter Anna almost died of spinal meningitis. Martina rubbed her with a bottle of fine wine they had brought with them, and she recovered.

The von Rapps were from Baden Baden. The family owned a grocery store and were fairly comfortable financially. Martina baked bread every day for their store and for their own family. She would always save a loaf for a starving French woman who had come across the border. She gave this to her free of charge, as the woman had no money.

The von Rapps thought well of the French. However, the French and Germans were traditionally enemies. Moreover, Napoleon III was rising to power, and Austria was at war with France in 1859. The king of Germany appointed Bismark prime minister in 1862, who immediately began mounting a large army against both France and Austria. The von Rapps did not approve. They were fearful that any sons they might have would be conscripted and forced to fight their neighbors.

They decided it would be best to emigrate. Ironically, in 1871, five years after the von Rapps emigrated from their native country, France ceded the Alsace Lorraine region to Germany for the first time, and there was a momentary calm on that front.

When they arrived in the new land, someone decided

Immigrants looking out on a new world — Back l. to r.: Anna (daughter), Martina and Augustine Rapp (parents), and Kate (daughter). Front l. to r. Louis, Adolph and Otto Rapp (sons). Photo taken 1880.

their name should be "Americanized." The title "von" was dropped, and just their surname was used.

Life was harsh for the Rapp family in the new land. They arrived in the United States in 1866, a year after the American Civil War had ended. The country was all torn up, and deeply impoverished. There was a great famine in the land, and many of the settlers starved to death. Like many of the pioneers, the Rapp family depended on potatoes for their survival. The Rapps settled briefly in Freebourg, Illinois. Their first son, Louis, was born there in 1868. Then the family moved to Missouri, where they worked as sharecroppers on the Morrison farm.

They had seven more children in Missouri. Adolph (my father) was born in 1871. Three years later the Rapp's had twins, Otto and Leo. Leo died of diphtheria when he was seven. There were two more girls, Emma and Mary, who also died of diphtheria. The three surviving boys were all three years apart. Then the two younger girls were born: Rena was born in 1882, and Carlie in 1884.

AUGUSTINE RAPP died in 1888. He became ill while going out one stormy night to fetch a doctor for his wife. Shortly thereafter, he died of Bright's disease, at the age of forty-eight. The three Rapp brothers were then fourteen, seventeen and twenty when their father died.

Shortly afterwards, Louis went to Texas to visit their cousin George Rapp. Then in 1889, he and his best friend, (the Suter boy), went to Oklahoma to race in the Cherokee Strip Race. The government was giving away land, Indian land. There was a big race from noon until dusk. The would-be land owners could ride anything: a horse, an oxen, a bicycle. Louis's friend staked a good claim and spent the rest of his life in Oklahoma. Louis didn't have a fast enough horse, and so he didn't get any land.

The Oklahoma Sooners got their name because they snuck onto the land and staked their claims before the race officially began. There was one story of a man who already had a vegetable garden growing when the first racers went past. Someone asked how he had grown his vegetables to a height of six inches already. He attributed it to the fantastic soil. He said they had sprouted in just ten minutes.

Louis went home for a little while after losing out in the Oklahoma land run. He soon had itchy feet again. He went west as far as Denver. When he got back to Missouri, he found out that his mother's health was failing fast. The family thought that it might be better for her if they moved to California, where the sun always shines. Louis had seen an advertisement in the farm magazine for a ranch in the Santa Cruz Mountains for only five hundred dollars. He went to California with his friend Lee Crigler to have a look at the place.

Louis purchased the property with the help of his brothers Adolph and Otto. They planned to bring their mother and three unmarried sisters to the sunny land. Just as they were packing up to leave for California, there was a flood in the Missouri lowlands. Martina was preparing to take in some of the refugees, when she suddenly suffered a stroke and died the same day.

The family went ahead with their plans to move to California. Adolph sold his heavy winter coat for a dollar. (As Mama always said at this point in her story, "He didn't sell it, he gave it away!") He later caught pneumonia after a trip to Monterey without an overcoat. He was extremely ill and almost died.

THE RAPP FAMILY came to California on the Southern Pacific Railroad and arrived at Wright's Station in the Santa Cruz Mountains. The three Rapp brothers had a foot race after getting off the train. One of them hollered, "The last one there pays for the beer!" One of the neighborhood gossips later said, "Those Rapp brothers must be a really wild bunch. They didn't walk, they *ran* to the nearest saloon!"

Their sisters didn't like the first property that Louis had bought. So Kate, Rena and Carlie returned to Missouri with their brother Otto.[21] They had seen the Crane Place, and

---

[21] The oldest daughter, Anna, was the only one of the siblings to have married by this point. She and her husband (cont'd.)

they told their brothers Louis and Adolph they would come back if they could buy that place. A year later, the brothers bought the Crane Place, and the three sisters and Otto made the long journey back to California.

The next morning after their arrival, at 5:12 in the morning on April 18, the famous 1906 earthquake hit. Although this is usually remembered as the "Great San Francisco Earthquake," it shook the Santa Cruz Mountains up pretty badly, much like the 1989 earthquake. The Crane house was mounted on stilts and it shook wildly. The bricks all tumbled down out of the two fireplaces. The water tower fell over. In the back of the property, several redwood trees snapped off like toothpicks and were hurled down the hillside. Some remained standing and grew back at odd angles.[22]

The Rapp women must have felt they weren't meant to live in California, but the brothers assured them they would repair the house and grounds as quickly as possible, and their sisters stayed on. Adolph enjoyed staying in the cabin, the oldest building on the property.[23]

Kate felt it was her responsibility to discipline the two younger women. If she thought they had done something wrong, she would turn all of the religious pictures towards the wall. She never told them exactly what they had done to displease her. Rena and Carlie would come in from their work on the farm and see the religious pictures all turned around. They would look at each other as if to ask, "What have we done this time?"

Kate had typhoid fever as a teenager, and she suffered some brain damage. Mama always referred to her as child-like, which was the kindest way you could put it. She had

---

(cont'd. from previous page)
had already moved to Whittier, California. Eventually they had six children together. Among the unmarried Rapps, Rena and Carlie were in their twenties, the three brothers were in their thirties, and Kate was in her forties. (Au.)

[22] When I was growing up, we called this grove "The Crazy Forest." (Au.)

[23] This cabin fell in 1989, during an aftershock of the Loma Prieta earthquake. (Au.)

been a beautiful young woman, and Will Baars, Papa's boyhood friend in Missouri, had been very much in love with her before her illness. They continued a correspondence after the Rapp family moved to California. A few years later, he came to California and asked Adolph's permission to marry Kate. Papa gave his permission. Aunt Kate and Uncle Will were married, and they lived right behind Highland School.

Kate and Will Baars never had any children. Will understood her unusual ways, and was always an excellent husband to her. Kate loved to ride on the roller coaster at the Santa Cruz Boardwalk. She called it the scenic railway. Once when Kate grew a little chubbier, there was a picture of her— a double exposure—which looked like she was sitting on both ends of a bench. Her husband teased her, saying, "I knew you were getting fat, but I didn't know you took up both ends of the bench!"

Kate and Will won a car one year by selling magazine subscriptions. Will had to buy a lot of the subscriptions himself. I have a picture of her standing in front of the car, which was festooned with garlands of flowers. Will thought it was so easy to win the first car, he borrowed money to buy enough subscriptions in order to win a second car. Unfortunately, not only did he not get the second car, but his debt was so high that he lost the new car — and their property, too![24]

RENA MET CHRIS JAUN when he knocked on the kitchen door at the Crane Place and asked if he could buy some vegetables. He had heard what a good garden the Rapps had. She was baking cookies and invited him in to sample some. They were married in October of 1911. The ceremony was performed in the Big Room. The priest came up from Los Gatos on the train. He brought an alter and while he was there, he also baptized my parents first two children, Elizabeth and Emma Mae.

---

[24] Kate wanted me to be named after her brother Louis, so I was named Margaret Louise. Mama said Kate always insisted on calling me by my middle name. I was only a toddler when she died, so I don't remember her. (Au.)

Seeing double — It looks like Aunt Kate is taking up both sides of the bench.

Rena and Chris lived most of their married life in Oakland, California. They had three children, Esther, Paul and Ruth. Their children were the first wave of cousins to visit us up in the mountains, before Janet, Phyllis and Virginia would come. Rena's children were closer to Clara, Adolph and Mary's ages.

Carlie lived with Louis and his wife May for many years. She was in her forties and still unmarried when May introduced her to John Everett. He was a widower in his sixties. Carlie and John were married in 1928. They lived in Willow Glen, California.[25] They never had any children. Uncle John did have a daughter from his previous marriage who lived next door to them.

John Everett had owned a large ranch in San Jose, and he sold off much of his land for development. A street in this section of Willow Glen was named after him—Everett Street.

May also introduced Otto to Lydia Lenihan. They were married in 1911. They lived in the Crane Place until 1915. Then they moved to the Blabon Place, another of the three properties the Rapp brothers had purchased together.[26] After a few years, they moved again, this time to Morgan Hill. They bought a prune ranch there, and also raised chickens, hundreds of them. I used to love to help Aunt Lydia gather the eggs. We gathered them up in buckets.

AUNT LYDIA was called our swearing aunt. I remember her as being very masculine, with a deep loud voice. Mama said Lydia had been very beautiful and feminine when she was young. She had long, flowing black hair, and she played the piano like a virtuoso. She worked as a secretary for Judge

[25] Willow Glen was independent of the City of San Jose, although it has since been absorbed by San Jose as a consequence of suburban sprawl. (Ed.)
[26] Mama and Papa had been living at the Blabon Place, but they moved into the Crane Place because they had a bigger family. Uncle Otto and Aunt Lydia didn't have any chidlren, and Mama and Papa already had their first three. Otto cancelled his debt on the Blabon Place by turning over his equity in the Crane Place to his brother Adolph. (Au.)

An unlucky prize — Aunt Kate's husband won this automobile by selling magazine subscriptions. However, it eventually cost Kate and her husband, Will Baars, their home.

Lieb in San Jose.[27] Mama attributed Aunt Lydia's masculinity in later years, when I knew her, to a hysterectomy she had in her twenties. In those days, that was an uncommon operation and they didn't give the patients hormones.[28]

The best loved story about Aunt Lydia is the time she and her hired hand Jake were driving with a load of prunes from the drying shed. Aunt Lydia was driving a Ford Coupe and pulling a little trailer with the prunes behind. They came to a railroad crossing, and without looking, Aunt Lydia barged right on through. They made it just in time, but a train snatched off the trailer with the load of prunes. "Gosh darn, that was close!" exclaimed Jake, turning white as a sheet. Aunt Lydia, dripping with perspiration, hollered, "Godammit! It wasn't any closer for you than it was for me!"

THE OLDEST AND MOST ADVENTUROUS Rapp brother, Louis, had been in love with Belle Crigler in Missouri. But he always believed that it was unrequited. After moving to California, he wrote his cousin Martin in Missouri and asked him if he thought Belle would come to California and marry him. Martin wrote back and said she was going with someone else and it looked pretty serious. She did marry that someone else, who was a doctor. But years later, when we were visiting in Missouri, she told us she had been in love with Uncle Louis, and she wished he had asked her himself. Also, she wrote once to my sister Clara, and said, "I could have been your aunt."

Louis met May Hemmingway Jaycox at a dance in the Skyland Hall. She was a divorcee, and was living on the Oettl Place at the time. She had a baby daughter by her previous husband, but the child did not survive infancy. Uncle Louis and Aunt May married in 1905. They settled into the first Rapp property, the Cuthbert Place. They had a good life together, but Uncle Louis could never forget his first love.

In the early 1900s, the mail for Longridge Road was

---

[27] He had been Mrs. Winchester's lawyer in his earlier years. (Au.)
[28] Who knows if the real explanation for her personality change was that simple? The important thing for historical purposes is that that was what the family and neighbors believed. (Ed.)

The Jaun family in the early '20s. Back row l. to r.: Rena Rapp Jaun and her husband Chris Jaun. Their children, from l. to r.: Paul, Ruth and Esther.

delivered to a row of mailboxes in a redwood grove near The Willows. Everyone who lived farther out had to walk to this row of mailboxes to get their mail. Louis was lucky, he only had to walk a quarter of a mile each way. Some people had to walk two miles. One day Louis walked down to the mailbox and there was a letter from Belle Knowles, formerly Belle Crigler. He was so excited he forgot to get the rest of the mail. He read the letter on the walk home. He was still reading it when he got back. May was furious! She asked, "What happened with the rest of the mail?" Uncle Louis hemmed and hawed. When May found out the letter that had so preoccupied him was from an old love, she was even more upset. It was a long time before she trusted him to fetch the mail again.

I SAW A LOT of Uncle Louis. He was my favorite uncle. I cut his apricots for drying at a rate of seven cents a box. He had a large strawberry patch next to the road, and across the road from our property. Everyone with a summer birthday got two baskets of strawberries. I always looked forward to those. Uncle Louis's strawberries were the best I've ever tasted in my life. He bordered his strawberry patch with sweet peas. Those sweet peas are still coming up, fifty years later!

Louis, who had been born to a farmer's life, was by nature an intellectual. On Sunday afternoons, he dressed up in his best suit and read all day. He had an extensive library, and especially liked scientific reading. He used to write to prominent men of the day, including Thomas Edison, Henry Ford and Albert Einstein.

Uncle Louis had a parrot named Polly. Polly had a large vocabulary. She would call the dog by name. "Laddie! Come boy!" She would laugh when we were laughing; she would bark when the dog barked; she would sing when Uncle Louis played the harmonica. Years after Uncle Louis died, I would still hear Polly when I passed by his house calling his name. "Louis! Louis!"

From l. to r.: May Rapp (Louis's wife), their parrot Polly, and Carlie Rapp. Carlie lived with Louis and May before she was married.

GENEALOGICAL CHART #2
THE (VON) RAPP FAMILY

Lawrence von Rapp
b. about 1800, Germany
m. a small redheaded woman

Augustine (von) Rapp
b. Dec. 15, 1839
in Baden Baden, Germany
1 of 12 children, 9 of them boys
immigrated to U.S. in 1866
d. 1888, Missouri

m.

Martina Bertsch
b. Jan. 18, 1840
in Baden Baden, Germany
immigrated to U.S. in 1867
d. 1905, Missouri

Anna, b. May 1863, Germany
m. Emanuel Jones
— Jaime, Kathleen, Mary, Louise, Leo, Emma

Katherine, b. May, 1865, Germany
m. 1911 to Will Baars
d. 1929

Louis, b. July, 1868, Freeburg, Illinois
m. May Hemmingway Jaycox
d. 1938, S.C.M.

Adolph, b. Sept. 1871, Prarie Hill, Mo. — 8 children see chart p. 268
m. 1908 to Emma Ingraham
d. 1966, S.C.M.

Otto, b. Oct. 1874, Salisbury, Mo.
m. Lydia
d. 1938, S.C.M.

Mary (d. in childhood)

Emma (b. 1881, d. in childhood)

Amelia Lorena (Rena)
b. April 17, 1882, Salisbury, Mo.
m. Chris Jaun, Oct. 12, 1911
d. 1961, Oakland, Calif.
— Esther, b. Dec. 18, 1912; Paul, b. Nov. 26, 1916; Ruth, b. June 24, 1917

Caroline (Carlie), b. April 29, 1884, Glasgow, Mo.
m. 1927 to John Everett
d. 1938, Willow Glen, Calif.

Note: (von) in parenthesis indicates that the family dropped it after immigrating to the United States.

Turn of the Century Vignettes

The Baritone

THE INGRAHAM FAMILY had just moved to Skyland in 1901. They went to the Skyland Community Church one Sunday. The church was just around the bend in the road from them. It was a little white church—only ten years old then.

The congregation was singing "Amazing Grace" when, all of a sudden, they became aware of a beautiful baritone voice rising above all of the other voices and filling the whole church with a marvelous operatic sound. Everyone stopped singing to listen to the sound reverberating throughout the building. It seemed as if it were coming straight from heaven.

They turned around in unison to discover the source of this outstanding voice. In the back of the church, a ragged old derelict stood, belting out this beautiful hymn with all of his heart.

After the service, the minister talked with him. The congregation crowded around. The minister asked him where he was from, and where he had received his vocal training.

Years before, the man said, he had sung with the New York Metropolitan Opera Company. He was now down on his luck, and just passing through the mountains.

A neighborly outing, c. 1906. Pictured l. to r,: Rena Rapp, Jeannette King, Carlie Rapp, Emma Ingraham, fiancé to Adolph Rapp (far right). The group travelled by horse and buggy to the top of Mt. Loma Prieta. This trip is not for the faint of heart, even in a modern automobile.

THE UNWANTED SUITOR

ONE DAY IN **1904**, when Mama was sixteen and Aunt Belle was nine years old, Mama confided to Belle that there was a country rube who kept coming into the Burrell General Store when he knew it was her shift. He would buy two cents worth of gum drops, and hold her captive with his talking for four hours. He was lovesick, and definitely had romance (of some kind) on his mind. Mama didn't want to complain to her mother, but she told her little sister. Belle had a solution. "I'll fix 'em," she said.

Aunt Belle took a bag of rice up into the attic, where she knew there was a knot hole right over the counter. Every few seconds, Belle dropped one grain of rice onto the unwanted suitor's head or face. He stood there swatting and slapping, until he decided to leave.

He never came back to pester Mama again.

AUTO REPAIR MADE EASY

IN THE EARLY DAYS OF THIS CENTURY, Henry Ford's Model Ts were a new sensation. Those who loved change, flocked to purchase one of these new "automobiles." Still, maintaining them was a different matter from the old horse and buggy, where a little grease on the wheels and a little hay for the horse power was all that was necessary.

One fine day, Clayton Jones, a notable Skyland resident, was riding through the mountains in his horse and buggy. A man was driving towards him in a Model T, moving in a halting, jerky fashion. It seemed that the engine was falling down.

Clayton Jones stopped and tied up the man's engine with a chain that he happened to have with him.

When he met the man a few weeks later, Clayton asked him how his Model T was doing. He replied, "Oh, that chain's holding up just fine." Apparently, he didn't feel it was necessary to make any further repairs to his automobile.

A TREMBLING MARRIAGE

BILL AND ANNA MARIE ADAMS moved from San Francisco to the Santa Cruz Mountains shortly after the 1906 earthquake. They were important members of the Skyland community in the early part of this century. Bill Adams was an active member of the Farm Bureau. Anna Marie gave many of the children violin lessons.[29] She had played with the San Francisco Symphony in her earlier years, even giving a concert with them in Mrs. Winchester's house for the dead Indian souls that that old woman believed were haunting her mansion.

---

[29] She was my violin teacher for one year. (Au.)

The Adams' marriage day was a notably rocky event. They were married in 1906—April 18, 1906. They were living in San Francisco at the time. When the earthquake hit at 5:12 in the morning, Miss Anna Marie Hadsell awoke, and quickly tried to escape her house. The piano was walking down the hall, and the walls were buckling wildly. She finally got out through a window.

When she got outside, there was Bill. He had come over to see if she had survived the earthquake. The momentary panic of danger must have inspired him to action. He said, "I've got our marriage license in my pocket. Let's go find a minister to marry us."

So they went down the street, and there was a minister and his wife, who was perched over a pot of beans she was boiling for breakfast. The minister agreed to marry them, and they all entered the church together, which was a bit of a mess from the recent trembler. That didn't bother Anna Marie so much as the fact that the minister's wife kept holding the dripping spoon from the bean pot throughout the brief ceremony.

The three San Francisco newspapers—the *Chronicle,* the *Examiner,* and the *Bulletin*—coordinated their efforts and printed a one-page newspaper about the earthquake. There was a society column with only one story: the Adams' peculiar marriage on the day of the Great San Francisco Earthquake.

COURTSHIP AND MARRIAGE

PAPA WAS TALL, DARK AND HANDSOME. He was a quiet man, and extremely proper. He was thirty-four years old when he and Mama met. He had just been in the mountains long enough for he and his two brothers to buy up three prime properties. The three ranches were close by and they owned and worked them together.

Papa looked around the new community and decided that he wanted to become an active member of it. He started by walking the two miles up the hill each Sunday to attend the Skyland Church. He had been raised a Catholic and the Skyland Church was Presbyterian, but it was the only church in the mountains, and it was a center of community life.

Mama was seventeen and she played the church piano every Sunday. Papa said she was just a slip of a thing then, weighing only ninety-eight pounds. Grandma started inviting Papa to Sunday dinner, which was always chicken. This soon became a weekly tradition. Papa introduced cards into the routine. They played whist, and somehow Mama and Papa always played on opposite teams. Papa almost always won. Mama said whenever Papa won, he would get a twinkle in his black eyes. This infuriated her and she would throw her cards down on the table. She would run upstairs and slam her bedroom door behind her, not to be seen for the rest of the afternoon.

After about a year of the church, chicken and cards routine, Papa got brave. He bought three ladies pocket watches. He gave one to his sister Carlie, one to his sister Rena, and one to Mama. He had each watch engraved with the woman's name. His courage must have faltered, because a little while later he wrote Mama this letter: "Dear Emma, I was going to ask you to marry me, but I guess I'm too old

89

Adolph Rapp (Papa) on Catalina Island, 1915. Although his hair was dark, his mustache was a startling red.

for you. My family doesn't live very long and I probably will die young, too. I won't be coming to see you anymore. Love, Adolph." Mama wrote him back: "Dear Adolph, Why don't you come and get your watch? Love, Emma." He followed her advice. Mama said when she met him at the door, he looked so forlorn, she fell into his arms and kissed him and they were engaged.

On December 29, 1908, Papa invited Mama to ride with him down into Santa Cruz in his horse and buggy. The winter day was short and the sky was grey. It looked like it might rain. They couldn't possibly make it all the way back up the mountain that same day. They had been planning to marry at the Skyland Church, but they decided to get married that very day. They couldn't stay in town a night without being married. They were married at the old court house by a justice of the peace.[30]

As they were coming out of the court house, they met J.J. (Joseph) Bamber. He was a wizened little man. He lived and worked up in the mountains as a Realtor, but came to Santa Cruz every month to have his newsletter printed which advertised properties for sale. He would include a joke or two and a bit of mountain news. With the spirit of an old newsman on the trail of a hot story, he asked Mama and Papa, "May I congratulate you?" Papa swelled with pride and said, "Yes, we just got married." Mr. Bamber leaped through the air and did an about face, shrieking, "I've got to stop the presses!" He had his newsletter, *The Realty*, reprinted and distributed in the mountains before the newly married couple returned from their honeymoon the next day. The mountain folks said it was the first time they'd ever read any real news in *The Realty*. The article read: "The illustrious and prominent Mr. Adolph Rapp married the charming and beautiful Miss Emma Ingraham." Mama and Papa spent their honey-

---

[30] This old court house was later converted to the Cooper House, which many Santa Cruz residents will remember as a popular local hangout filled with shops and a café. It was severely damaged in the 1989 earthquake, and was later demolished. (Ed.)

Mama holds Emma Mae on her lap, and Elizabeth is squeezed in between Mama and Papa, 1912.

moon night at the Bayview Hotel in Aptos.[31]

Papa had bought an organ for his sisters when they lived in Missouri. When they moved to California, he paid to have it shipped around the horn. Then, after he married Mama, he paid his sisters Carlie and Rena the three hundred dollars he had originally paid for the organ and bought it for Mama. It was a most appropriate wedding present, as her piano playing on Sundays had originally brought them together and Papa knew how much she loved to play hymns. At the Crane Place, Papa's wedding present to Mama was the only piece of furniture to occupy the room we called the Organ Room.

PAPA PURCHASED THE BLABON PLACE, on November 24, 1908.[32] He and Mama lived there the first seven years of their marriage. They lived in a cozy little cottage, and pretty soon the babies started coming. Mama was assisted in the deliveries by her mother. Of course, Papa was on hand to boil water! Elizabeth was the first of many beautiful children. She resembled Papa, with his dark hair and eyes. He was so pleased with his first born that he sat up rocking her all night.

Two years later, Emma Mae arrived, a fragile little girl with red hair. She was so delicate Mama said she didn't

---

[31] It is still operating in 1995, eighty-seven years later. (Ed.)

[32] Adolph Rapp purchased this property from John William and Jennie Ray Taylor, who had recently immigrated from England. They had just purchased it themselves that year, on January 14, 1908, from Francis Brimblecom.

Brimblecom acquired the property from Julia Blabon in 1907, in a court ordered auction. He had taken her to court because of an overdue mortgage in 1906, and purchased the property that August. Her husband had recently died, and she was unable to redeem the property by the following year. Brimblecom sold the parcel just five months after acquiring it, at a profit of nearly $100, a tidy little sum in 1908.

Julia Blabon had purchased the 20 acre parcel from the F.A. Hihn Company ten years before her loss, in May of 1897. So although the Blabons only owned the parcel for ten years, around the turn of the century, old timers in the mountains still refer to it as "The Blabon Place." The Rapps eventually sold it to the Fidels, whose property it bordered on. The Fidels later sold it to the Lowes, who own it to this day. (Ed.)

The Blabon Place — The young family in front of their first home. Mama, Papa, and their first two girls, Elizabeth and Emma Mae. They had just shingled the house and built in a bay window when this photo was taken, in 1914.

The girls in their pretty white dresses. Emma Mae and Elizabeth, l. to r. Here they are posed in front of the cottage at the Blabon Place, 1914.

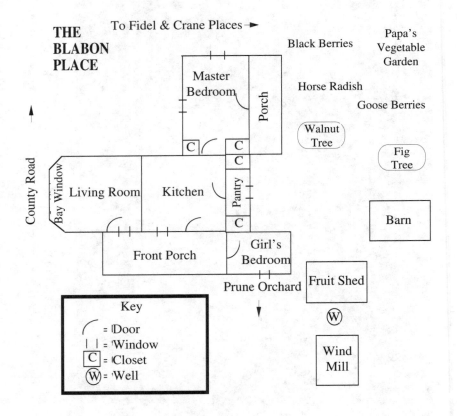

THE BLABON PLACE

To Fidel & Crane Places →

Black Berries

Papa's Vegetable Garden

Master Bedroom

Porch

Horse Radish

Goose Berries

Walnut Tree

Fig Tree

County Road

Bay Window

Living Room

Kitchen

Pantry

C

C

C

C

Barn

Front Porch

Girl's Bedroom

Prune Orchard

Fruit Shed

W

Wind Mill

Key

⌐ = Door
| | = Window
C = Closet
W = Well

Based on a sketch by Emma Mae Lydon

expect she would be able to raise her. She was allergic to most milk, even her mother's. Luckily they discovered that she thrived on goat's milk. As she was the second girl, Mama decided to call her "Sister."[33]

Four years later, Clara arrived. She was the first of the "triplets," as Mama referred to them, because they were all born so close together.

Next came Adolphus, the second red-headed baby and the first born son. We called him "Brother" for obvious reasons. The whole community adopted the nickname. Once, when he was older, he was walking down a street in Los Gatos and Uncle Louis hollered out to him, "Hey, Brother!" Brother was embarrassed because he figured people must think he belonged to some kind of extreme religious group.[34]

Two years later, Mary was born. She was their first blue-eyed blonde. Mary was goodness personified. Mama said Mary's sweet nature and sunny outlook resembled her mother Susan's. Mary always wanted everyone around her to be happy.

She was a lethargic little girl, and would easily drop off to sleep. One day, Uncle Will Baars ran over her with his Model T. She was lying asleep on the road, and he thought she was a dusty old rag. Fortunately those Model Ts were raised up pretty high and Mary was not seriously injured.

Mary didn't learn to talk until Mama went to the hospital to have her next baby. She was already four and she had gotten along all that time with sign language. For instance, she just pointed at a faucet and grunted, rather than

---

[33] This nickname did not stick to Emma Mae as she got older, possibly because Mama and Papa had many more daughters. (Au.)

[34] The nickname "Brother" stuck long into adulthood. He eventually dropped the "phus" from his given name. Once, when she was young, Emma Mae said, "My father's name is Adolph without the 'phus.'" Now in his seventies, Brother is trying to get everyone to call him "Adolph," and he frequently cites this story with Uncle Louis as an example of how embarrassing his long-lived nickname became for him. But since he was called "Brother" throughout the period covered in this book, that's what he will be called in these stories. (Au. & Ed.)

saying "water."

Mama was in the hospital for two months when her next child, Frank, was born.[35] Mama had an infection. The older children forced Mary to learn to talk while Mama was in the hospital by not giving into Mary's grunts. When Mama came back from the hospital, Mary ran to greet her. "Oh Mama, I'm so glad to see you! I missed you so much. Don't ever leave me again!" she shrieked. Mama liked to rehash this story at family gatherings. At this point, my husband would usually interrupt and say, "And you haven't stopped talking since, have you Mary?" Mary did love to talk, but she always considered how her words might affect people. Mama called her the family peacemaker.

THE FIRST TIME Mama and Papa were separated for any length of time during their long marriage was in 1922, when Mama went to the hospital in San Jose to have Frank. Mama was in the hospital for two months with serious complications. She had a kidney infection, and almost died. The long separation was difficult for both Mama and Papa. He visited her in the hospital as often as he could, and they exchanged many letters. They were still very much in love after fourteen years of marriage. Here are a few of the love letters they exchanged which attest to this:

> Wright's, Calif.
> May 30, 1922

Dear Wife,

I will write you a few lines before I go to work this morning. We got through howing over at the other place yesterday, but I am going over there this morning to sulphur. We have ben having good growing weather. Fruit is growing fast. I arto be thinning out my plums but there is other work I will hafto do first.

I haven't suckered my grapes yet. Otto came up from Morgan Hill the day before yesterday. He was here last night.

---

[35] He was the first of the children to be born in a hospital. (Au.)

The "triplets," c. 1921. From l. to r.: Adolph, Jr. (Brother), Mary and Clara.

He said Lydia and Carl were coming Sunday. He brought the dogs with him so I guess he will stay all summer.

Well, I thought I would get a phone message by now. It seems you have ben gon a long time. It's the longest since we have been married. The children are getting along fine and I am to as far as the work part is concerned but it's not lik having your sweetheart with you to love and be loved.

With love and kisses,
Adolph

Sunday Morning

Dear Husband, It was only yesterday that you were here. So there's really little news to write about. I'm writing more to kill time than by reason of news. It's a beautiful morning, and the grounds here are just like a park. I'm in the rear of the main buildings. They have a beautiful collection of song birds in an enclosure. They are singing so loudly just now. I didn't rest any too good last night, but I feel more comfortable this morning. Last night I was glad that I was here, but this morning I wish that I was home or that some of you were with me. Most everybody here are without any one of their own family so I guess that's what makes them all so friendly.

After you went away yesterday, I went into the diet kitchen and they were nearly through serving supper to the bed fast patients. I've been allowed to butter the baked potatoes and they were nearly through. I told them I had been detained. However I finished the job for them. One of them laughed and said, "Oh yes, we realize that you were busy entertaining your "sweet heart." She said that was all right though. A good one was a nice thing to have. I told her that was what I thought. If I ramble on much more you'll think that I'm trying to write a real love letter.

Well, I hope you come next Sunday and bring a string of the children with you. I don't see any reason why you couldn't bring them all along. You could get a room where that old lady lives who has the rooming house, out there where I have stopped so much. She has a room with two beds in it. You and Brother and Mary could use one, and Elizabeth and Sister and Clara could use one. She's a dear old motherly woman. She would not think anything out of the way. I always have an old fashioned visit with her, every time I stay there, and she always remembers me.

I want Sister to call Mrs. Napier and order two yards of black grossgrain ribbon and fix her new sailor hat. I enjoyed the dainty eats you brought me. This morning I had a big dish of strawberries for my breakfast. I cooked some of them down into jam so they'd keep while I'm here. The good things you brought me to eat will just about last me while I'm here, I think. I been faring better since I've been allowed access to the kitchen. For supper I had bread and gravy, and prunes with milk, and soft boiled eggs. I always enjoy my breakfast here, more than any other meal they serve. I like everything they serve but it was those potatoes that got my goat. Especially the way they were served. They never have served pie, and a small piece of cake is served for Sunday dinners. May's cookies were a real treat. When any of you see her, you tell her I said so. When you come again, Adolph, you bring me my birth announcement cards. They're around our dresser in our bedroom, I think. I also need ten cents worth of "one cent" stamps to use in order to mail them. Bring a comb, too, I need one so badly. And a watch. Maybe Ida will loan me her wrist watch. It's so handy. My watch is in the glass cupboard, in the dining room, on the top shelf in the salid dish. I hope you're all well and I'll see you before very long again.

Mama

June 13,
Tuesday morning

Dearest husband I wont get your postals until after mail time, so I'll write you a few lines. I can't write much. I feel badly this morning. I've had constant pain in my back and on my left side ever since midnight last night. I've had hot water bags on the place that hurts. They gave me

The first orange crop — The children each hold an orange to demonstrate that these are the first from the new tree. From l. to r.: Eloise Fidel, Clara Rapp (standing), Emma Mae Rapp, Marie Fidel, and Elizabeth Rapp. c. 1918.

medicine twice for my pains. I think it helped some—but still, I have considerable pain. And the baby is six days old this evening. With the other children I didn't have such heavy pains after that many days. I suppose they will pass away in time.

But I fear I wont be strong enough to come home Sunday. I'll write again tomorrow.

With love,
Emma R.

Wright's, Calif.
June 24, 1926

Dear Sweetheart,

We got home all right. We got stuck on the Boston Hill. The water leaked out of the radiator and of course the engine got hot. We got nearly to the top before she stopped but it took about half an hour before we made it to the top. We filled it with some ice in the radiator before she would pull. We would go about a foot at a time and would put a chunk of wood under the wheel so we finely got up.

I told your dad it was a good thing he had me along. He said you bet he said I earnt my ride and supper and a big dish of ice cream and he shurly gave me a big dish I guess about a pinte.

Brother and Mary and Clara and Frankie all went up about an hour ago to get some ice cream. I gave them a dime apiece. They also picked some blackberries to trade grandma for some ice cream to take home.

Arno was hear this morning to see me about the hauling. He said if he could get enough hauling that he would get a larger truck. He said his father had ben up to the city to see the cooperative cannery. They told him they wer mailing out checks to pay of them notes which sounded good. They also said we get some more money out of our last years pears, which sounded good also. But you know they have made promises before which they dident always keep.

Mrs. Stephans just called me up wanting me to come over to discuss about hiring the teacher at 3 o'clock this afternoon. I told her I would be there. Well I guess this is about all of the news. Well Sweet Heart, I hope it wont be long before you will be home again because I need you more than you think, but don't worry, be chear ful and time will pass. I will be down Tuesday or Wednesday or if something happens sooner.

With Love and Kisses,
Adolph

Frank was the second son, and also the second blonde, blue-eyed baby. He was a friendly little boy. When he was four or five years old, he would run to greet Mama's car, following her into the garage. This made Mama anxious.

Once, Mama was driving the Maxwell along the dusty road above The Willows. Elizabeth and Emma Mae were arguing in the back seat. Frankie, a two-and-a-half-year-old boy, was sitting there quietly minding his business. Mama heard a thump. She didn't dare look around because she was a very cautious driver. She asked, "What was that thump?" Elizabeth said, "Oh, Frank just fell out." Mama slammed on the brakes and looked around. There was Frankie screaming at the top of his lungs and running to catch up with them. He was covered with dust. (This was before the roads were oiled. They were six inches deep with dust then, and that had cushioned his fall. Also, Mama only drove about five miles an hour.)

The next child, Sammy, was stillborn. Papa took him home from the hospital in a shoe box. Papa, Grandma Ingraham, Elizabeth, and Emma Mae buried Sammy in an unmarked grave in the back of the property. When Mama was in her seventies, she asked Elizabeth to show her where Sammy's grave was. It was between Papa's vineyard and the madrone grove.

I arrived two and a half years later. Mama was hospitalized with complications. Her last three births were difficult, and it was a good thing she was able to receive medical attention. The nurses phoned Papa. (I had arrived just after he had left to go back to the ranch.) Mama wanted to be sure Papa knew the baby had red hair. Papa just

Papa holds baby Margaret. Standing right is Mary. Photo taken 1927.

chuckled. I was their third redhead. It was said that we got our red hair from Papa's moustache. (Although he had dark hair, Papa had a red moustache, creating a startling effect.)

The last time Papa ever drove was when he took Mama and me home from the hospital. He hadn't learned to drive until he was in his fifties. He was naturally a very nervous person. It was about twenty-three miles up to the ranch, but Mama and Papa stopped in the little village of Los Gatos to rest after going about ten miles. The last thirteen miles were winding and narrow, and Papa needed to relax a bit before starting the drive up the mountains.

Then Salvadore appeared! Salvadore worked for Papa on and off, clearing some old redwood stumps from the land. He used dynamite with a heavy hand. Salvadore was a short man, about five feet tall. He was from Russia. He had kinky, curly hair and wore thick glasses with metal frames. He always wore aluminum shoes about six sizes too large as they were the same price as the smaller ones. He wrapped his feet in burlap sacks to fit the boots. He spoke seven languages, all of them loud, and punctuated them with lots of swear words.

When he ran into Mama and Papa in Los Gatos that day, Salvadore had just returned from the Alaskan gold mines. He proceeded to remove his money belt and lay out all of his gold nuggets on the sidewalk. This caused quite a stir.

When he put them back in his pouch, the crowd dispersed, realizing this was not a giveaway. Salvadore tagged along to the sweet shop with my parents. That's when he noticed me. He cooed, "Pretty baby," and made clucking noises. When we entered the sweet shop, he shouted, "Get this baby all the *@*($#& ice cream she can eat! And the mother, too. She just had a baby!"

SALVADORE

"LADY, if you want redwood stumps grubbed out, say redwood stumps and not hazelnut brush or poison oak!"

With that, Salvadore walked away. Mrs. Garike had advertised in a San Francisco paper for a man to grub out hazelnut brush and poison oak. Salvadore answered the ad. He took the train to Wright's. Mrs. Garike lived seven miles from the depot, and she came in her horse and buggy to pick him up. When she showed him the so-called brush, it turned out to be large redwood stumps. He remonstrated and walked away, feeling he had made the long trip under false pretenses. She went after him, and evidently they came to some kind of an agreement, as he grubbed the redwood stumps for her.

Papa met him and asked him if he would grub out some redwood sumps at the Crane Place after he finished his job for Mrs. Garike, who owned the Hoops Place.

Salvadore worked for Papa awhile before going off to Alaska to do some gold prospecting. This was about forty years after the gold rush, but there was still some individual prospecting going on. When he came back from Alaska, he continued grubbing out redwood stumps for Papa. He was always paid by contract so he worked on his own time. After two or three months, he would go hoboing. He usually left by the shortest route, right straight through the woods. Where he went was a mystery. He always returned suddenly, and without notice.

Salvadore was certainly a thorough worker. Once Mama asked him to clean out the garage. He did just that. He cleaned it all out and burned everything: the old victrola, the old recorded cylinders, all of the old books and other memorabilia. Mama never asked him to do anything extra again.

He just stuck to his stump project until he finished.

He worked for Papa ten years. I remember him blasting dynamite in the back of the property until I was six or seven. He was a meticulous worker. He cleared all of the dirt around the stump with a spoon before blasting. He would study a stump for hours, preparing for the big explosion. He used dynamite with a heavy hand. He liked to hear the blast. Mama would cringe whenever she heard one of the explosions, hoping that one of her smaller children wasn't too close by. He named each of the stumps after a priest. He saved the biggest and toughest one for last, calling it "The Pope."

SALVADORE SPOKE SEVEN LANGUAGES FLUENTLY, and he could recite an entire mass in Latin. His manner of speaking ranged from the profane to the very cultured. He would never use a small word when a bigger word was available. Hence: excavate, rather than dig. He was entirely self-educated. He had only been to school one day in his life. He had received a spanking, and vowed never to return.

After he was grown, he travelled all over the world and had many exciting adventures. He told us one story about the time he went to Buckingham Palace and asked to meet the king of England. He was arrested and fined the equivalent of ten dollars. He did not have the money so he was put into jail. His time was only valued at six cents a day, so he was jailed for six months. He said after that he hated the king of England!

Mama was very curious about Salvadore's past, and she would question him about it. He only gave succinct answers to her questions. She asked him what was his last name. He said it was Ober. She asked him if he had any brothers and sisters. He said he had a twin brother who had died. Mama was dying to ask more. But he refused to answer any more questions.

He was well travelled, and had obtained most of his knowledge from the people he worked for. During his life, he had worked for a doctor, a lawyer and a priest, among others. In his younger years, he had been a sailor.

While living in Chile, Salvadore took a job on a ship. What he didn't know was that the ship was doomed. The woman who owned it wanted it to sink so she could collect on the insurance. She manned it with several sailors from different nationalities. No two spoke the same language, or so she thought. What she didn't count on was that Salvadore spoke all of these languages.

She had the ship loaded with manure, loaded all on one side so the ship listed to that side. She sent it out on a stormy sea. She didn't reckon on Salvadore speaking all of the seven languages that he did. He was busy running from sailor to sailor, giving them instructions to man the lifeboats.

The ship *did* sink, but the sailors survived! The woman was very surprised to see them all come back to port in the lifeboats. She tried to get on their good side by putting them up at a very expensive hotel. Salvadore said he had never seen such luxury!

SALVADORE WAS FROM RUSSIA. He was a very slight man, only about five feet tall. He had long, kinky curly hair and long bushy whiskers. He never shaved, but sometimes used clippers. His clothes were always too big. He felt he was getting a better deal that way because he got more material for the same money. He would tie up his oversized pants with a piece of clothesline cord. He always wanted to get the most for his money—hence he wore aluminum boots that were too big because they were the same price as a smaller size. He would wrap his feet in burlap sacks until the boots fit right. As a child, I wondered if the lenses in his glasses were so thick for the same reason. Salvadore always wore the same old leather cap with a visor. He never thought it needed to be replaced as long as it was all in one piece. It didn't matter what it looked like. He would often remove his cap with a flourish, when greeting someone.

Salvadore had a good sense of humor, but did not take well to teasing. He was hot tempered. When Brother was ten, he loved to tease Salvadore. So one day Salvadore assumed that Brother had snuck into his shack and cut off his boot straps. (He later discovered that the rats had chewed them

The only known photo of Salvadore in existence. Here he is regaling Amadeus Tarquinio with one of his tales in Italian.

off.) He flew into a rage and threatened to kill Brother.

One day, Mama was in the packing house making crates. She had a hammer and nails in her hands.[36] Suddenly she heard screams coming from the cherry orchard in the back of the property. It sounded like a little boy. Mama hollered for Jack, "Hurry up, Jack," she screamed, "Salvadore's killing Brother! I'll bring the axe! You run faster than I do, so you run on ahead!"

When they got to the cherry orchard, they discovered little four-year-old Frankie screaming and carrying on because Brother was making him bring in the goat.

Salvadore wasn't really a child hater. When I was a little girl, he used to swoop me up and call me Margaritta Louisa. He loved to push me up the long steep driveway in a wheel barrow. To me, he was like a little gnome coming out of the woods. He would always appear when you least expected him. I would look up from one of my childhood games and *behold!*, there was Salvadore. He would always stop to dance a jig with me, or give me a piggy back ride. Sometimes his eyes would mist over and his voice would become gentle just at the sight of me. He was not much taller than I was, but he had a booming voice which could easily have frightened a small child. I knew I could trust him though, because my parents were always glad to see him. He made Papa laugh and they all treated each other with great courtesy and respect.

My sister Clara wrote a story about Salvadore for her English class at Los Gatos High School. It was so good they read it over the radio. My parents invited Salvadore to come and listen to it while it was being read. Midway through the reading, he circled his temple with his forefinger and said, "Somebody must have wheels in his head!" Salvadore was a very secretive man, and didn't like being talked about over the radio.

Salvadore used to pay Mama a dollar to drive him into town. He would also treat her to dinner and a movie, but he

---

[36] This was a common sight. Mama loved to make things with wood, such as packing crates or furniture. (Au.)

wouldn't sit with her because he didn't think that was proper. He would point to her table and tell the waitress to "Get that woman over there any *¢∞%#* thing she wants to eat!"

For the few years that Mama drove the 1932 Buick coupe, which had a rumble seat, Salvadore would sit up on the edge of the seat because he was too short to see out if he were to sit down in it. My cousin Floyd Hurney said it was the funniest thing to see Salvadore go riding by, sitting in this precarious position, looking all around to see what he could see.

One day, Mama took him to a Charlie Chaplin movie. It had the by-now-famous scene where Chaplin is having a tooth pulled by a quack dentist who winds up pulling them all. Mama said Salvadore was sitting a couple of rows in front of her, and he was even funnier to watch than the moving picture! It affected him so much he lifted his cap and swore; he pulled on his beard; he had to turn around to shield his eyes; he was practically climbing over his seat by the end.

Salvadore walked the twenty miles round trip to Soquel once, in order to fill up a jug of wine. He didn't realize until he got back that night and poured a couple of glasses for himself and Papa, that the jug he had taken had had kerosene in the bottom of it. He and Papa both spat out the liquid in unison.

SALVADORE HAD THE CONSTITUTION OF FIFTY MULES. He used to love to pick mushrooms and eat them, but one day he ate some toadstools instead. This would have killed most people, but Salvadore just got a very bad stomach ache. Mama took him to the doctor and got him some medicine. He was supposed to have a tablespoon every two hours. Salvadore wasn't used to these fancy new city doctors and their medicines. He figured that if a little was good for you, a lot would be better. Why spread it out a tablespoon at a time? So he drank the whole bottle! This really made him sick. He moaned and groaned something awful. But he still pulled through.

Clara and Brother used to stay up late every week and listen to the radio show "Amos and Andy." There was only one set of earphones so they would take turns listening, and then tell the other one what had happened. One night Salvadore came in very hungry. Clara and Brother had left a plate of spaghetti on the table. He hollered, "Get me some tools!" But they couldn't leave "Amos and Andy!" Salvadore was so hungry he grabbed a pair of scissors and started in on the spaghetti. He couldn't find any "tools," as he called silverware. He called a fork "a pitchfork," a spoon "a shovel," and a knife "a dagger."

Salvadore always made his presence known when he was hungry. One night he showed up at Aunt Ida and Uncle Will's place. He knocked at the front door but nobody heard him because the kids were all upstairs in bed and Aunt Ida and Uncle Will were eating a late night supper of spaghetti, after the house had quieted down. Salvadore was very hungry. He lost all patience and walked around to the back of the house, where the kitchen was. He poked his head in through a broken window pane right above the kitchen table and boomed, "Godammit, isn't anybody home?"

Just as Uncle Will was lifting a fork full of spaghetti to his mouth, Salvadore's face appeared right in front of his face. Uncle Will turned white as a sheet, and Aunt Ida told Mama it was as if, "Salvadore had taken ten years off of Will's life!" Will was naturally a very quiet man, and something like this was bound to shake him up.

The next day, Salvadore asked Mama if there was anything wrong with her sister Ida. Mama said she didn't think so. Salvadore said, "Well she looked white as a sheet when I went by their place last night."

One summer when Papa was sick, and just before Elizabeth and Jack returned from Canada, Salvadore acted as a straw boss during the fruit harvest. He would do anything for Papa. This he did without pay.

SALVADORE WAS ALMOST EIGHTY YEARS OLD IN 1946, when I introduced him to my future husband. Salvadore relished the opportunity to speak Italian with my fiancé, Amadeus. I was extremely shocked and disappointed when I found out what Salvadore had said to him. He said, "If things don't work out

with this one, there are plenty of Italian girls in San Jose."
There was a large Italian community in San Jose, and later I
reasoned that maybe he assumed an Italian would want to
marry another Italian. But I still felt a little betrayed by the
man who used to push me up the steep hill in a wheel barrow
when I was three years old. It was the last time I ever saw
Salvadore.

Salvadore lived like a wild thing. He would make a
hut using two prune trays, leaning them together like an A-
frame. This way he could cook his beans and bacon on the
campfire and the smoke would all blow away. He would
cook everything in one pot: beans, bacon, berries. As he said,
it all went to the same place anyway. He ate at the tables of
the mountain folks when he got a hankering for a real home
cooked meal.

Sometimes he would appear at our front door and pay
one dollar for all the pancakes he could eat. Usually this was
about two dozen. Once he stopped in and asked Clara for a
couple of pancakes. She said, "You mean two dozen?" His
pride was so hurt, he wouldn't eat any.

He didn't bother about things like property lines. He
squatted on 'most everybody's place up in the mountains at
one time or another. During some of his travels, he told us he
had had a real roof over his head, moving into an abandoned
shack which he called a hobo hotel. By an amazing coincidence, Salvadore had actually spent some time squatting in
the house Mama had lived in as a little girl, across the road
from Mrs. Winchester.

He was still living in a mobile A-frame in the mountains when he was in his eighties. He became ill and the
Welfare Department discovered him living, as they would
say today, the life of a homeless person. They hospitalized
him and set him up in a boarding home.

But Salvadore didn't last long "in captivity." He died
shortly thereafter, they say of pneumonia.

LAUREL

GEORGE NAPIER *WAS* the town of Laurel. There was a tiny train station. He was the station master. There was a grocery store. He owned the grocery store. There was a post office. He was the postmaster.

Laurel was only about five miles from Skyland. Since the post office was a fourth class post office, his pay was the amount of the postal cancellations. Because of this, he could deliver the groceries through the postal system at no extra cost to himself. I have never heard of this being done before or since.

The timing was perfect, as the morning train was going towards Wright's, the next station on the line. If Mama needed something for the noon meal, or dinner, as we called it then, all she had to do was call Mr. Napier before eight in the morning. Mr. Napier would package it and ship it off to Wright's. Uncle Will would pick it up at Wright's, along with the rest of the mail for the Santa Cruz Mountains. Mama could have it on her table in time for dinner. Laurel was only five miles away from our house, but with the winding roads and the five mile an hour driving limit Mama imposed on herself, the trip required an hour.

When we needed a lot of groceries, Mama would make the trip to Laurel in her Maxwell, and later, when I remembered it, in the Hudson. It was as exciting as a trip to San Francisco would be for me today, probably more so. If I was lucky, the train would be coming in, letting off its blast of steam and a loud whistle!

Mr. Napier was a very generous man. He would give the children each their own bag to fill up with candy and other sweets.

I still remember the many different smells in the

store—the smell of the oiled wood floor in the main part of the store, the smell of the kerosene and sawdust in the adjoining room, where he kept the bulkier items. We got kerosene for lighting our lamps, and rope and chicken feed from that room. He carried many hard-to-find items, like horse collars and flat irons. Each year when we were paid for our fruit harvest, we would go to Laurel and really stock up. The children would take turns going so there would be room for all of the supplies in the car. Mr. Napier would give each of us children an extra large bag to fill with goodies when we paid our bill.

He was so generous that he carried many families through the depression. He told Brother he had $38,000 still on the books over the forty years he ran his store at Laurel.

Before opening the store, he had gone on the Klondike trail in 1898 with James Bassett, Clayton Jones, Julius Josephat and James King, four prominent Skyland residents.

Mr. Napier had his store from about 1898 to 1938. The train stopped running on February 8, 1938. Heavy rain washed out the tracks. The timing was just right. Mr. Napier was getting older, and he was ready to retire. That was the end of another era.

Emma Mae Remembers
the 1910s

I ASKED MY SISTER EMMA MAE about her earliest impressions of life in the days just before and after World War I, especially her memories of early family life and growing up in the Santa Cruz Mountains. Emma Mae was born in the mountains on June 12, 1911. She told me the following:

"I remember Mama when she was very young. She was almost twenty-three when I was born. She was petite and full of energy. I remember her laughing and crying. She was very loving and playful. She would sew dresses for Elizabeth and me. She loved to play the piano for us and sing and dance.[37]

"Mama had taken lessons from a Miss Mille when she was a teenager in the Santa Cruz Mountains, and practiced on her mother's Fischer piano when she lived at home with her."

Emma Mae said Mama also played the piano for the Skyland Church and for the Highland School programs. Emma Mae continues:

"Mama would join Elizabeth and me in playing house, and having tea parties and other games. I remember bedtime. We said our prayers. I remember one night there was thunder and lightning and we had to get up and move our bed. The roof was leaking. Aunt Belle and Aunt Ida were

---

[37] I remember Elizabeth telling me these same stories when I was a little girl, and I felt a little envious as I never knew Mama when she was young, and she seldom played the piano anymore when I was little. (Au.)

very young and they would sometimes come and stay and take care of us. They would play dress up and have tea parties with us.

"I remember visiting the Woolcotts, who were our neighbors. Mrs. Woolcott was a dear woman. She loved children and would save bird feathers and bits of cloth for them to play with when they visited her.

"I remember Mama running with me from a coiled up rattler that was under a prune tree. I remember train rides through the mountains and going to Catalina Island when I was four years old, and going on the glass bottom boat. I used to like to go shopping with Mama, when I was older and Grandma Ingraham no longer had the store at Skyland, due to her ill health. We would go the five miles to Laurel then.

"Most of these memories were before I was four years old, and Clara was born, on July 11, 1915. After Clara was born, we moved in the fall of that same year to the Crane Place. We lived on the Blabon Place until I was four. I loved it! That was my home, and it was a cozy little two bedroom cottage. When we moved to the Crane Place, it was huge. The rooms were big! Some of the rooms were very dark and it was cold. It was impossible to heat it all with just the wood stove in the kitchen and the wood stove in the living room. Mama and Papa exchanged properties with Uncle Otto and Aunt Lydia.

"Mama liked the Crane Place as it was closer to the school and to Skyland Church, and to her parents where they would go every Sunday for dinner."

Mama called Elizabeth and Emma Mae her twins, and Clara, Brother and Mary her triplets because they were born closer together. Brother was born on October 28, 1916, one year after Clara. Mary was born on May 25, 1918. Mama was always tired after that. Besides having the three babies, there was lots of work on the farm, and she had a large house to take care of.

Emma Mae went on with her narration: "I remember our buggy rides with Mama and Papa to church on Sunday mornings, and then on to our grandparents to Sunday dinner. Their property adjoined the church. The air was clean and

A quiet evening at home — Papa reads the paper and Mama does needle point, while Elizabeth and Emma Mae play. This interior shot of the Blabon Place in 1913 is typical of a Skyland home before electricity came to the mountains.

fragrant from the many plants and trees. There were wild flowers and berries to gather in the springtime. I loved the smell of the freshly cut tree at Christmas. Papa brought it in the night before and Mama put the toys around. Such fun in the morning when our mother played with us. She would set up for the parties with our new dolls and dishes. Mama spent much time drawing and writing on the blackboard that our Uncle Chris made for us. She even taught us the alphabet before we went to school.

"We had no inside plumbing to clog up, or electric wiring to go haywire. We all worked together on the ranch. At first Mama and Papa would turn the prunes and sack them, while Elizabeth and I played nearby. Later we helped too. Mama would use the worn out gunny sacks to make a play house for us."

Emma Mae said Mama described her seven children thus:

Elizabeth:	Inspirational
Emma Mae:	Faithful
Clara Belle:	Courageous
Brother:	Faith in himself and family
Mary:	Peacemaker
Frank:	Healer
Margaret:	Loving

Emma Mae went on to tell of staying overnight with Grandma and Aunt Kate. This was another point of envy for me. I don't remember my grandparents or Aunt Kate. I do love to hear about them though.

"Mama had us stay with Grandma or Aunt Kate during heavy storms. She was afraid of lightening and falling trees on the way to and from school. We liked the upstairs bedrooms at Grandma's where we could listen to the raindrops. Grandma was an excellent cook. Aunt Kate's place[38] joined the school yard, and was across the road from the

---

[38] Aunt Kate's house fell on October 17, 1989, during the earthquake. (Au.)

Ernest Griner, Belle Ingraham's husband, in France during WWI. He was an Army doctor.

Louis Wicht in his WWI uniform. His sister Annie Wicht stands at his side. The Wichts were another early Skyland family, and many of their descendants still live in the area. The photo was taken April 28, 1918.

church and the store. Aunt Kate went to the Catholic church in town, and she would take us to Mass on Easter Sunday. These were part of our extended family, and Mama certainly needed helping hands.

"The Crane Place was called 'Vista Del Mar.'[39] It had been a parcel of land from the Hihn tract, a split off from a Spanish land grant.[40] There was a stage coach road to the Gransby tract of land on the back hillside that joined our place.[41]

"Our closest playmates were Marie and Eloise Fidel. Their mother, Mrs. [Emma] Fidel, told Mama fascinating stories. One that entertained and amazed Mama was the story of Marie's appendectomy on the dining room table. Dr. Knowles brought his surgical staff to the home for the emergency. The appendix ruptured after it was lifted from the wound, a remarkable recovery for those days. Many people died in those days from a ruptured appendix.

"Mrs. Fidel helped Mama with my feeding problems. I ate pearl barley and drank goat's milk. Later Elizabeth and I both loved to play in the Fidel's attic.

"The Carlson's were good friends and neighbors. They lived a mile towards Skyland. Elizabeth was a good friend of Ruth Carlson.

"The Wraggs were from England. Winifred Wragg was a good friend of Mama's. My first impression of God was from a man who seemed very close to the one he called

---

[39] There is a magnificent view of the Pacific Ocean from this property. (Ed.)

[40] The Crane's property appears to be land that L. Reis purchased after it was split off from Spanish Ranch, according to County records. However, many people who remember the Crane Place from the old days believed that it was once part of a Hihn tract of land. The next property over, the Blabon Place, was purchased directly from the Hihn Company by Julia Blabon. Since Mrs. Blabon still owned that property when the Rapps acquired the Crane Place, she was likely the source the story regarding the Hihn tract. (Ed.)

[41] The Crane Place is on Longridge Road, very near to where it goes down to the Spanish Ranch Road. (Ed.)

his master. Mr. [Tom] Wragg was an ordained minister.[42] His services reached the hearts of everyone, and especially the children. Sometimes he would gather us around him. Sometimes he would send us out to play when he wanted to talk to the adults. I was fascinated with his facial expressions when he prayed. He seemed to be shedding tears of joy. His prayers seemed to be mostly of thanksgiving. Years later, I had a chance to thank him in a little way for what he did for me. Mama stopped at the nurse's home with Mr. Wragg in her car. He was hemorrhaging from a tooth extraction. I was able to control the bleeding with an ice pack."

I also remember the Wraggs as very warm, loving, and religious people. The Wraggs married in England in 1907, and left just one week later to move to the Santa Cruz Mountains. Their close friends, John and Jennie Taylor, who at that time had just purchased the Blabon Place, wrote to them about how beautiful the area was. They especially stressed how healthy the mountain air was, as Winifred Wragg suffered from terrible asthma. The Taylors met the Wraggs at Wright's station. The Wragg's quickly established themselves in the mountains, and raised their only child Marian there.

Mr. Wragg loved to read, and he had a large library. He frequently invited me in to read his daughter Marian's books. She was a friend of Emma Mae's and had grown and married by the time I came along. As an interesting aside, Marian's brother-in-law was Charlie Chaplin. Marian's husband Jesse Harris had a half-sister named Mildred Harris, who married Chaplin.

Emma Mae continues: "I remember the big flu epidemic after World War I. We wore masks to school. That didn't keep me from getting the flu. Most of us up in the mountains pulled through with the exception of Ruby

---

[42] According to Marianne Wragg Harris, her father Tom Wragg was not actually an ordained minister, but a church elder who conducted services when needed. However, it is easy to see how many people in the mountains at that time might have had the impression that he was ordained. (Au.)

Winifred Wragg and her daughter Marian. The Wraggs moved to the Santa Cruz Mountains from England because they thought the healthful mountain air would be good for Winifred's asthma.

Hanaford. She was the daughter of the first postal delivery man.

"Mr. [Earl] Hanaford delivered the mail from Wright's station. He had a team of mules and made a lot of noise as he tore down the road. He carried a pint flask with him and by the end of his route he was pretty tipsy. All of us children learned to scramble out of his way when we heard him coming.

"Our mailbox at that time was lined up with about a dozen others near The Willows, in a picturesque redwood grove. There was a water tank to sprinkle the dusty roads and to water the thirsty horses in the watering trough. There was also a swimming pool, which was a dammed up watering hole. All of this was supplied by a very active creek.

"Mama taught me responsibility. I helped with all of the babies as they came along, and later worked for a family in Campbell for my room and board while I went to high school. One of the children there was handicapped.

"I then went on to nursing school and became an RN. Except for a few years off to raise my son Michael and my daughter Mary, I did nursing all of my life until retirement."[43]

---

[43] Emma Mae received her RN license in 1934. She is 84 now, and still occasionally nurses her many relatives. (Ed.)

Flu prevention? Elizabeth and Emma Mae model the flu masks popular with school children during the 1918 influenza epidemic. Most of the children who wore the masks got the flu anyway.

Ruby Hanaford (standing) was the only victim of the flu epidemic in the Santa Cruz Mountains. Hanaford, daughter of the first mailman in the mountains, suffered an ironic fate. After graduating from nursing school, she went over to Europe in WWI as a nurse. She returned to the mountains after the war, only to catch influenza and die.

Seated is Belle Ingraham, her childhood friend. The occasion is the graduation of the two women from Mt. Zion nursing school. In those days, the design of a nurse's cap and the pin worn in the cap were unique to each nursing school. In this way, anyone who knew the significance of the cap and pin could tell where a nurse had trained.

THE LURE OF MR. KING'S ORCHARD

THE CHILDREN growing up around Longridge Road all considered our neighbor James King to be a mean old man. He was a real old-timer, having come to the mountains in the early 1880s. By the time Mama's children were growing up, he was quite elderly.

Mr. King's property bordered the county road for several hundred feet. He had a grove of orange trees next to the road. His house was also close to the road.

An exciting adventure for the children involved trying to pick a few oranges and get on past his house, without a serious confrontation with Mr. King. What the smaller children didn't realize was that, if they were coming from the north and going by his house first, this alerted Mr. King of the possibility of their taking a few oranges. He would sneak out his back door, grabbing his cane on his way. As the children did the anticipated deed, Mr. King would come roaring through the grove, waving his cane and bellowing! This scared the holy pie out of them. I'm sure this was a bigger thrill than if they had met with the Wicked Witch of the East. This was real flesh and blood rage!

The only hope of remaining unnoticed was to come from the south, from the direction of the Crane Place, take a few oranges and quickly retreat. This often worked. But one time Clara and Brother went over with their little red wagon, intent on doing the dastardly deed. They had put several oranges into the wagon when they heard Mr. King coming through the trees, ready to scare them to death. (Actually this was part of the fun of the whole thing, as all the families up there had their own orange trees. But for some reason Mr.

King's oranges always tasted better!) Clara promptly jumped in the wagon, on top of the oranges and spread her skirt over them...covering up the evidence just in the nick of time. Since Mr. King never actually laid a hand on the children, Clara and Brother got away with it.

Another time when Frank and our cousin Bob Hurney were both ten years old, Frank told Bob this wild tale. He said, "If you steal any oranges from Mr. King, he will tie you to a tree with a rope and beat you with his cane!" Bob ignored this and went on picking a few oranges. Frank didn't take any, thus making the story more believable.

Frank and Bob went back to our place next door. A few hours later that summer evening, the boys both looked up and spotted Mr. King coming over the hill from his place. He had a rope and a cane! Bob took off as fast as his young legs could carry him down the hill toward Steffie Fidel's place. He ran so fast and so far that he lost both of his shoes.

When Aunt Ida came to get Bob, the truth of the matter came out. Mama made Frank go look for Bob, and also help him look for his lost shoes. What neither of the boys knew was that Mr. King's cow had gotten away, and he brought the rope to lead it home. And of course, he always walked with a cane.

HOLY CITY

FATHER RIKER AND MOTHER LUCILLE came to the Santa Cruz Mountains in 1918. They founded the small "religious" community of Holy City on the road between Skyland and Los Gatos, which was the old highway before Highway 17 was built. Coming from our place, it made a great stop for refreshments and to get gas. After all, the drive to Los Gatos was fourteen miles! Holy City was also a shorter distance to drive if you only needed to get a few groceries, or to get a hair cut for six bits (75¢).[44]

Holy City was a toylike little town, complete with a grocery store, coffee shop, service station, post office, barber shop, and even a movie theater and bottling company. Prices were reasonable. An ice cream cone was a nickel, and a huge hot dog with coffee or a soda was only fifteen cents.

Joe Albert, the manager of the grocery store, was called "Holy Joe." He told us that Father Riker tempted anyone who was homeless but looked like he had a bit of sense to come and work for him. He paid them a dollar a week and all they could eat. This was during the depression, and that was a tempting offer to anyone who had fallen on hard times. The only trouble was, it was tough saving enough money to get out of Holy City, since you were primarily working for your room and board.

I never did understand Father Riker's religion. He seemed more like a religious bigot to me. He hated blacks, Jews, Orientals and Catholics. This was interesting because he later converted to Catholicism at the age of ninety-four. He said he was an excellent candidate because he had been

---

[44] By the late 1930s, the two Ingraham General Stores and Mr. Napier's store in Laurel had closed. (Ed.)

Holy Cow! Holy City Press burns down! — A series of mysterious fires destroyed much of the remnants of this ghost town in the late fifties. Here, in 1960, the all-important (from Riker's standpoint) Holy City Press burns to the ground.

living a celibate life for the past ten years.

He had had his exploits with the fairer sex in his younger years. In 1909, he was accused of bigamy. Two women claimed to be his wife, and neither of them was Mother Lucille, the woman he moved to the mountains with.

When they moved to the Santa Cruz Mountains, Father Riker and Mother Lucille claimed to have lost their marriage license in the 1906 earthquake in San Francisco. Mother Lucille dressed in a nun's habit. This was very unusual, considering they were not Catholic, and Father Riker was not to embrace the Catholic church for another forty-eight years.

Father Riker was a Nazi before his time. When Hitler rose to power, Riker hailed him as one of the greatest leaders of all time, possibly the greatest since Christ.

Father Riker was a real doom and gloomer. He put up signs throughout Holy City, all basically saying the same thing. Something to the effect that the world was coming to an end and mankind was doomed. He also had a row of doors on a facade which was maybe a foot deep, leading nowhere. They were all locked and each one had a sign on it. "This door was locked in 1920. It will not be reopened until 1944." Or even, "This door will never be reopened."

One Christmas, he put up a bunch of little churches and Santa Clauses. For a penny, you could peek through a peep hole in one of the little churches and read some religious saying, inevitably a pretty depressing one. These did so well that he left them up all year 'round.

Father Riker ran for governor on several occasions. He always had large banners strung across the roads entering and leaving Holy City. This was just two bends in the road. The banners read, "FATHER RIKER FOR GOVERNOR."

Father Riker professed to revere womankind and motherhood.[45] Once, while expounding to Mama, Riker said, "All I am and all I have I owe to my precious mother."

---

[45] This was very interesting as his so-called religious colony had only male converts. Other than Mother Lucille, all the people I ever saw working there were odd-looking single men. (Au.)

Mama said, "Give her two bits and you won't owe her anything."[46]

---

[46] Riker is not exactly a common surname; however, it should ring a bell for *Star Trek* fans. Apparently this is not a coincidence, according to Tom Stanton, who runs Holy City Art Glass out of one of the few remaining buildings on the site. He said one of the creators of the *Star Trek: The Next Generation* series lived in Los Gatos, where he learned about the curious history of Holy City. He was so fascinated that he named the fictional character Riker after the real-life character Father Riker. (Ed.)

LIZZIE'S STORY

WHEN GRANDMA AND GRANDPA INGRAHAM celebrated their fiftieth wedding anniversary on October, 1926, I was three months old. I was not included in the family picture since I had the whooping cough. Uncle Ernest, who was a doctor, diagnosed it that day. He took one look at me and said, "That child has the whooping cough." Later that same day, he drove into Los Gatos and got inoculations for all of the children. The rest of the family was in the picture. They had all come from miles around for the celebration.

Dinner was on the table and Grandma had just said, "All we need now is for Lizzie to show up," when Lizzie called from Holy City and said she needed a ride. She had come all the way from Scott City, Kansas. Uncle Ernest went out to pick her up.

Lizzie was an unwelcome guest at this celebration. She had had a falling out with her brother Hiram and his wife, Susan, a few years earlier. Great Aunt Lizzie wrote my sister Emma Mae a letter in 1922 which helps explain why.

July 14, 1922
Scott City, Kansas

Dear Niece,

I got your kind letter a long time ago. Your card a few days ago. I am all alone in this world, no one to love or care how to get along. I have been burnt out 4 times in my life, twice when brother knew. Fred gave me calico for a dress. Your uncle Jasper gave me ten yards of muslin for underclose. Brother Hiram nothing. Brother Jim nothing.

So when my brother Fred died, I lost the only protector I had. I had to mortgage my home for everything that I got and cant make much money. It ain't like it used to be. I use to be able to work and soon could get started again.

I did not expect Susan to give me money but I did expect her to help me as much as a towel or a kwilt. I lost the hous and all the contents. I had nothing to keep hous with or do with.

When you are out in the world and prosperous, everybody gives you a wellcome hand. But when misfortune comes, the world turns a back to you. Then family love should show itself. If your sister Elisabeth is sick or burnt out, give her a welcome and helping hand. She will feel the loss, but she will know she has a friend that will cheer her in her loss.

In this, Susan is to blame. They had no money that they could share, but she had an over plus in her home. She could have shared a few articals. Belle boasts she had bed close for 5 beds once and only use one. So you see, there is an over plus all so.

I am glad you are all well. What is the baby's name? Crops are poor here.

I can't expect to come to Calif. very soon. How is all the folks by this time. Be a good girl. Help your Mamma all you can. Do your part by your parents. Some day you will be glad for it.

From your aunt,
Elizabeth Tyler

Aunt Lizzie must have known that Hiram and Susan would hear the critical things she was writing about them to their granddaughter. This, combined with Lizzie's sour personality, probably started the feud. Nevertheless, Lizzie felt it was important for her to come to their fiftieth wedding anniversary four years later.

AFTER THE ANNIVERSARY CELEBRATION, Lizzie stayed on, and on, and on...She had grown very bitter and she nagged and complained, whined and picked, and was just too miserable to have around. Finally Grandma called Mama and said,

Hiram and Susan Ingraham celebrate their golden anniversary. Back row, l. to r.: Hiram Ingraham, Elizabeth Rapp, Papa, Mama. Second row, l. to r.: Elizabeth (Lizzie) Ingraham Tyler (with hand on hip), Susan Ingraham, Clara Rapp, Ida Hurney (holding her son Floyd), Belle, her husband Ernest Griner, Emma Mae Rapp. Front row, l. to r.: Bob Hurney, Mary Rapp, Virginia Griner (holding her mother's hand), Phyllis Griner, Adolph Rapp, Jr. (Brother), Frank Rapp (in back of Brother), Barbara Hurney (in front of Brother).

"Emma, *please*, I'm dying; won't you *please* come and take Lizzie off my hands and let me die in peace?" (This was not an idle complaint. Grandma did die four months later.)

Mama had just assumed the responsibility of running the farm because Papa's health seemed to be failing fast. When Susan called Mama and told her to take Lizzie off her hands, Papa had just been given three years to live, and Mama was in the middle of harvesting the grapes. They had to be picked, packed, and shipped to San Francisco. Mama knew that her mother must be desperate to call her up at a time like this.

Mama dropped everything and went up the road to Skyland to get Lizzie. Mama kept Lizzie, but only for a short while. She quickly realized that Lizzie could send her over the edge. One time, when Lizzie was complaining (she would hardly stop for breath sometimes) Mama said, "Lizzie, didn't you ever have a good time in your entire life?" Aunt Lizzie stopped cold. She thought and thought. Finally she said, "Let's see, there was one time...." We never found out what that one time was. When Mama finally came to the end of her rope, she shipped Lizzie off to San Francisco with a load of grapes. Mama never saw her again!

I laughed uproariously when Mama told me this story. I was twelve and it was the first and last time I ever heard Mama tell it. (I don't imagine it was one which she was too proud of.)

A few years later, I told Elizabeth about hearing this story. She said, in her serious way, "Aunt Lizzie had a plenty to be miserable about." Then she told me Lizzie's story, because she wanted me to understand how my great-aunt had become so bitter.

AUNT LIZZIE went to work for a farm family after leaving the orphanage. She had to work very hard. If she had finished with the cleaning, one of the smaller children needed seeing to, or she would be called upon to help out with the farm work. She always had plenty to eat, so she was better off than she had been in the orphanage.

Through her brother Hiram, she met Jasper Jewel,

Susan's older brother. Lizzie married Jasper and they moved to another part of Iowa. They homesteaded a parcel of land and built a cabin. They had a baby girl named Lydia.

One day Jasper was digging a well, when the well caved in and buried him alive. Lizzie didn't know what to do. She didn't have any money or any family of her own close by. She asked the neighbors down the road, Mr. and Mrs. Shields, if they could loan her ten dollars in the emergency, and watch her baby until she returned. She went away to try to borrow some money from her brother Hiram, or another family member.

When Lizzie returned, she found the Shield's cabin boarded up and the family gone. They had taken Lydia with them. The family didn't have a child of their own, and Lizzie guessed rightly that they had wanted one badly enough to kidnap hers.

Lizzie spent the next forty years looking for her daughter. In the meantime, she remarried and they adopted two children, a boy and a girl who were full brother and sister. She didn't want to split them up, knowing how hard it had been on her and her brothers.

Every time Lizzie got a lead, she would scrape together a few dollars and go in search of her daughter Lydia. Finally, after a tip from an old neighbor, Lizzie found Lydia in Denver, Colorado. Her name had been changed to Jenny Shields, and her married name was Martin. Mr. and Mrs. Shields had adopted Lizzie's daughter, saying that she had been abandoned. They had never been able to have a child themselves, and they had lavished everything on Lydia. They owned oil wells by this time in Oklahoma, and they were quite wealthy. Jenny was forty years old by the time Lizzie found her, and she owned a stylish little millinery shop in Denver.

When Lizzie came to Grandma and Grandpa's fiftieth wedding anniversary, she had been abandoned by her second husband and her adopted children. She had become so intolerable to live with.

Thirteen years later, in 1939, Mama got a letter from Jenny. Mama and Lizzie hadn't spoken after Mama sent her off to San Francisco with a load of grapes. Jenny helped bring us up to date. Ironically, Jenny was trying to contact Lizzie, who had abandoned all correspondence with her by this time. We never knew why. My guess is that Lizzie was jealous of the family that raised Jenny, as she seemed to love them as her own parents. Jenny sent a picture of herself, and she could have been Mama's twin sister. They were double cousins. Jenny's mother was Mama's father's sister, and Jenny's father was Mama's mother's brother.

Denver Colorado
13-19th 1939

Dear Cousin Emma Rapp;—
I sure was glad to hear from you and I wrote to Belle and your girl but I guess they knew you wrote to me and that was enough anyway. It is hard to write as busy as a nurse is and a Dr wife is but I know you two are busy as can be.
I got my new teeth a week ago. I was in bed two weeks after Xmas with the flu and bronkitis. I wrote to mother today but I suppose she will send it back as usual or upbrade me for writing but I feel I will do all I can do write that is what I think is write [right] as long as I live anyway. Most of the people you mentioned in your letter I never heard of before. Say cousin, do you really know what nationality we are I never knew? It snowed and stormed all winter here and nearly broke us up buying coal all winter. Times are awful hard here for us at least. Mr. Martin has been well this winter. Do you know where any of Jim Ingrahams children are? Or how one would go about to find them? You have no idear how much chear your letter brot me it sure did. One cant hire any help here as everone is on relief and get fiftyfive dollars and clothes given them and hospitalization free and dental work free and only eleven days a month to work at five dollars a day and can keep a car and work quite a bit on the side if they are not caught.
The largest oil wells in North America is on my fathers farm in Oklahoma. It has sixteen other wells and the big well produces 80000000 feet of natural gas a day and over

64000 barrels of oil a day but my girl sold it for four thousand dollars and was totaly broke before she was twentyone years old together with my foster mother and father that is legally adopted father and mother. If I had my own way I would have never sold the old home place for I loved it. It was known and is known as the Walker Well at Crescent Okla. And it is located in Section 33 town 17 Range four west Logan County Okla.

Well I got to terrible much work to do I will close for this time and will when I get more time to write. To me you feel like to me as if you were my loving cousin and all her kind family. I am so proud to be relatives of respectable people like you folks.

I couldn't help but be proud of mother when I heard she was keeping boarders for a living and still working to keep off the pencion. I am not sure but a lady that lives near her brotherinlaw she says boarded with mother in Scott City last year. Write to me when you can I remain with lots of love to you my cousin Emma Rapp

Jenny Shields Martin
Denver Colorado.

As far as I know, that was the last time Mama heard from her cousin. I wish we had Jenny's daughter's name so she could fill us in on how the rocky relationship between Lizzie and her daughter evolved.

Grandpa's Mail Order Bride

G RANDMA'S HEALTH FAILED rapidly after their fiftieth wedding anniversary. From October 1926 to February of the following year, her health had declined so much that Grandpa took her in his Model T to Aunt Belle's and Uncle Ernest's house in Stockton. He was a doctor and she was a nurse.

As they were loading up the car, Ida said, "Help Mama, Emma." Mama stepped forward to help her mother up the high step into the Model T. Grandma refused her help, saying, "I ain't dead yet, Emma." Susan died that night in her bed, in Stockton, on February 14, 1927.

Hiram was lonely and sick after Susan's death. One day he picked up a magazine which advertised women who were looking for a husband, commonly known then as mail order brides. Grandpa must have thought this was the answer to his prayers, so he sent away for Annie. Annie arrived at Wright's Station wearing a black hat with a red feather, and carrying an overstuffed suitcase. They married shortly thereafter.

The Ingraham sisters were not pleased. They cherished the memory of their mother, Susan. In fact they were all still in mourning when their father remarried. To add insult to injury, Annie wanted them to call her Mother. Mama was thirty-nine and had seven children. Annie was only a little older than Mama. Grandpa was seventy-one!

What Grandpa really needed was a nurse. His health declined rapidly, and he died two years later. He left the Skyland and Burrell stores to his wife Annie. This caused much bitterness among the family members, who hadn't liked her from the beginning. Annie felt the sisters should pay for his funeral since they were his natural kin. The sisters thought Annie should pay for the funeral since, as his wife, she would inherit the property. The sisters finally got their way by not attending the funeral service. They went and sat in the shade of a tree on the edge of the Soquel Cemetery and watched from a distance.

After that, Annie packed her suitcase and boarded the train at Wright's station with hardly a backward glance.

Through correspondence, she sold the two stores to Mama who had a deep sentimental attachment to them.

Jan 24, 1930

Dear Emma, I received your letter yesterday. You did not say a word weather you would be willing to help me save the Burrell property from Bashford or weather you would reather I would lose it—how do you expect me to save $500.00 when I get $250 a year for rent—the $200.00 is not enough for the Funeral expences alone the $400.00 will leave me just $166.00 to save torde redeaming Burrell & it will come to you girls in the long run I think the offer you made me was terable besid I will half to meet you in Los Gatos that will take money as I will have to hire a woman in my place while I am gone I think I can make it with the $400.00 I pay the undertaker 234 as I will get $100.00 next summer of my own from another sorse I wont borrow any if I dont half to I have a few $ in the bank tord the note but it will strip the bank clear to make up what is laking on the 200 you offered besids other creditors are after me for old debts he had before I knew him. Now be reasible think it over I would to God I could get it somewhere else I shure would not ask you you will never no what it cost it was for your father that I asked I would starve to death before I would come to any of you for my self and it is to save Burrell for you girls not for me now if you want Burrell when I am gone come across with the $400 & if you dont then I will take the 234 & you will never get a cent more out of Burrell & I will meet you any day you set in Los Gatos with the deed you bring the morgage but dont tell any one as other creditors want there pay to yours truly

The Burrell General Store, once the center for telecommunications in the mountains, went for the sake of progress. The County leveled it in order to widen Summit Road.

> Mrs. H.D. Ingraham
> 87th Ave
> Oakland Calif

Mama wrote Aunt Belle regarding these business negotiations:

Wed Jan 29, 1930

Dear Bell,

I wrote you a letter about a week ago, but you haven't answered my letter. I presume you got it.

Well this pen is simply terrible and it is just about time for the mail so between them both I can't write much.

But I got another letter from Anna—I rote back and offered $200.00 and this is the answer to my letter.

So I rote back and told her I'd give her the $235.00 and if that was O.K. meet me in town next Friday Jan. 31st.

So of course I don't know what she'll do next, but I guess I soon will know.

The Italians are telling some other people who have rented the little cottage from <u>them</u> that they own the place and have for 5 years. They pretend that they are starting up a store again soon. Well anyway, they're making themselves right at home there. Time's up so will close

Love Emma

But Mama hadn't seen the last of her business dealings with her stepmother, as witnessed by this letter:

April 14   30

Dear Emma,

I am writing to let you know that I cant get in touch with Loui Greco. I wrote to the tenant on Skyland told him to see you if not do as you like but you had better get him off before the year is up. Loui comanced to pay rent May the first 1929 and you no it so dose Egglestons, Gadmans, Clowes and all the neighbors up there. Tom Collney the cowboy drove the car to Oklahoma. Johnny Wood and Mr. Green moved us. I guess you wont have much trouble he doesnt own the place and I told him not to put any improvements on the place nor to fix it up except to cut the weeds around the house.

Yours Truly
Mrs. Anna Ingraham
Oakland, Calif.

Papa, a good businessman, didn't see the sense in Mama buying her father's properties from Anna. The two stores were defunct by then. However, he knew how much it meant to Mama to keep them in the family. Mama did rent the Burrell store to the telephone company for several more years. They paid her just enough to cover expenses. Anna had already rented the Skyland property to the Greco family when she sold it to Mama. Mama continued to have the same problems with the tenants that Annie had had.

The Grecos lived in San Francisco, but they vacationed at the Skyland property on weekends, holidays, and summers. They would go for months and months without paying the rent of fifteen dollars a month. Then, when Mama was at the end of her rope, she would go and pay them a little visit.

These were Italians on vacation, so naturally they showed us their most boisterous side. This didn't set too well with Mama. This was her first brush with Italians.[47] The Grecos wallpapered her dear old house that she had lived in when she was growing up. The only thing was, each strip of wallpaper was a different pattern. They also had red streamers hanging from the center of the ceiling. They were a large family, and several of their older daughters had children, so there were a lot of them.

When Mama showed up to collect the back rent, they would invite her to dinner. After joining them at their groan-

---

[47] She developed a prejudice towards them, which I later had to buck when I introduced her to my husband to be, who is very Italian. (Au.)

ing board,[48] Mama was always in a much better mood.

Louis Greco was an importer from San Francisco. Mama would always come home from one of these meals loaded down with embroidered bedspreads or some such thing.[49] Mama would bring her latest plunder into the house. When she showed Papa what she had gotten for the last six months rent, he would sniff and say, "How are ya' going to pay the taxes with them?" All Mama would have to say was, "But Adolph, they are so pretty," and Papa would smile.

I never thought of Mama as a business woman, but when she was dealing with the Grecos, who were on her property, she was forced to write up a business agreement. One time they had not paid the rent for eighteen months. (This was in 1934, the heart of the depression.) Mama devised this elaborate plan whereby they would sell her their furniture and household goods for the back rent. The agreement went like this:

KNOW ALL MEN BY THESE PRESENTS:
That Louis Greco, 236 Guttenburg St., San Francisco, California has sold to Emma B. Rapp the list of household goods following for three hundred ($300.00) to be paid in rent of house at Skyland belonging to Emma B. Rapp, whose P.O. address is Wright's, California.

Mr. and Mrs. Greco of the above address S.F. have volunteered to sell their household goods and furniture complete as are at the present date which is Sept. 15th, 1934 to Sept 1st 1935.

But because of the good care taken of the place, the rent will be extended two months more making the furniture completely paid for in rent by November 1st, 1935. Mr. and Mrs. Greco agree to accept the balance due them on furniture in the form of rent as explained above. The list of furniture consists as follows:

---

[48] This is an old fashioned slang term for a table loaded with food. (Au.)
[49] I particularly remember a lavender one with long purple fringe that stayed on my bed for many years. I liked it so much it inspired me to paint my bed purple. (Au.)

4 bureaus
1 counter for store
1 showcase for store
1 ice box
1 davenporte
2 cook stoves
1 parlor set of
1 settee and 3 chairs
to match
1 corner chiffinere
Dishes which are
89 strait plates
15 cups and saucers
18 stew pans and kettles
4 coal oil lamps
2 frying pans
1 roaster
2 roast pots
1 table and benches on porch
1 9x12 wool rug
9 small rugs
1 gasoline engine in basement
and water pump
1 grind stone
6 double beds with mattresses
and bed springs and covers complete as are
5 single beds and mattresses and springs (cover)
1 cot
4 stand tables
5 dining room tables
14 dining room chairs
2 rocking chairs
1 portch chair

I don't ever remember seeing all of this furniture around, so I don't know how this was resolved.

The Burrell store went for the sake of progress.[50] In 1939, the store was sitting empty. The telephone company had moved out and attached themselves to Ma Bell. The County called us up and said they needed the property to widen the road. They had the power to force Mama to sell them the property through the right of imminent domain. But Mama was a fighter. Mama and I moved into the store and claimed we were living there. I was thirteen at the time. Mama was trying to claim that we were a hardship case. The County wasn't falling for this one. They forced her to sell. She received fifteen hundred dollars for the property.

Louis Greco had stopped renting the Skyland store by this time. Mama began to focus all of her daydreams onto this property. She started to think about moving back there in her old age, if Papa went before her. This would likely be the case, as he was seventeen years older. Papa was very upset when he learned of her plan. He couldn't believe she would leave the wonderful home he had provided for her to return to her father's home. Without consulting her, Papa put the Skyland property up for sale.

Mama was furious when she discovered he had gone behind her back like this. This caused a major rift in their relationship. Even after Mama agreed to sell, she was still upset with Papa for a long time. Later on, she came to understand that it was very important for him to know she would continue living at the Crane Place, even after he had gone.

---

[50] It wasn't on the same site as The Summit Center is at present, but it was somewhat near there. The old Ingraham General Store in Burrell was right across from the old grammar school on Summit Road, where the widened road now takes up much of the old site. (Au. & Ed.)

Entrance to the "New Jerusalem Colony", circa 1930s. A pack of dogs guarded the gateway to "Mother" Alice's retreat.

Everyone's Crazy but Me and Thee...

A ND SOMETIMES I WONDER A LITTLE ABOUT THEE. My family did seem to be one of the relatively few "normal" ones in the mountains; and that, of course, is strictly a matter of opinion. Even we had bats in our belfry. (Literally. They flew out of our attic at dusk, and returned just before dawn.)

But seriously, the isolation of Skyland in the early part of this century created an atmosphere that was ideal for mystics, misers, ascetics, and other reclusive individuals who did not conform to the expectations of mainstream society. Mama loved to recount stories of the many colorful characters who had been her neighbors. Many of these people were long gone by the time she first told me about them in the 1930s, although some of them still walked the mountain backroads while I was growing up.

Above all, there was Mrs. Benninghoven—alias "Mother" Alice—who everyone said thought she was the mother of Christ. She lived at Skyland near the General Store. She would walk the winding mountain roads wrapped in white sheets and carrying a long crooked staff. Sometimes she rode a white horse. She always had a pack of dogs following her. The sign in front of her property read "New Jerusalem Colony."[51] As far as I knew, she never had any converts, other than the dogs.

---

[51] There were two alternate names for the mystical colony listed in the deed when the Benninghoven's sold some property in 1906. Listed above the Benninghoven's names were "Brotherhood of the White Star," and "Order of St. John of Jerusalem." The sign reading "New Jerusalem Colony" was definitely in front of her property in the
(cont'd.)

The Skyland rumor mill had it that Mrs. Benninghoven was hypnotized by a travelling Hindu while her husband was away, and that she never came out of his spell. When her husband, Ernst, returned home, she wouldn't let him back into the house. He camped out on the front porch a few nights. He tried pleading with her, reasoning with her, anything. Then he realized the situation was impossible and left. He moved into another property they owned nearby. When her husband died, Mrs. Benninghoven still wouldn't let him into her home. His casket sat out on her front porch until the neighbors took him away and buried him.

Another story explaining Mrs. Benninghoven and her ascetic ways also circulated. In this version of the tale, the Benninghoven's went to the holy land for their honeymoon, and she came back a changed woman.[52]

There was a constant feud between Mother Alice and Grandpa Hiram. She used to tether her horse on his Skyland property. He asked her to cease and desist, but she kept doing it. One day, he found her horse tethered on his property and took it into Santa Cruz. One of the bailiffs tethered the horse outside the old courthouse and went inside. He got the judge to come out and take a look at it. Grandpa was claiming that the horse was malnourished. It was awful skinny. While they were in the courthouse, Mrs. Benninghoven came along and rode the horse back up to Skyland. She and Grandpa never had anything to do with each other after that.

Once, when Mama and her sisters Belle and Ida were young, they visited Mrs. Benninghoven at her place in the

---

(cont'd. from previous page)
1930s, however, as evidenced by the photo on the opposite page. It is possible that during the ensuing decades after 1906, Mrs. Benninghoven's name for her colony evolved. (Ed.)

[52] John Young, who was reporting in 1934, wrote that *Mr.* Benninghoven was the leader of a strange religious cult in Skyland, and that his wife was carrying on his work just a few years after his death. Young did not give his source for this information, and so the story remains shrouded in mystery. However, residents who remember Skyland in the '20s and '30s all confirm that the couple lived apart for most of their married lives, in separate Skyland properties. (Ed.)

Mrs. Benninghoven, alias "Mother" Alice, at ease on her front porch, in her reclusive hideaway.

woods. Mother Alice served them cheese sandwiches—
moldy cheese on moldy bread. Mama and her sisters, trying
to be polite, nibbled on the sandwiches, avoiding the moldy
bits. When Mother Alice sat down with them and took a
sandwich for herself, she said, "Oh! These are moldy!" She
tossed it over her shoulder. The dog ran over and sniffed it.
He evidently didn't like what he smelled. He lifted his leg up
and peed on it.

Another time, when Mama was grown and had her
own family, she took Emma Mae to visit Mother Alice. Mrs.
Benninghoven met her at the door and asked, "Do you have
an axe to grind?" Mama assured her that it was a friendly
visit. Mother Alice said, "No one ever comes just to visit me.
But if you're sure you don't have an axe to grind, come on
in."

After that, Mama, who had a high tolerance for
strange behavior, would entertain Mrs. Benninghoven about
once a year. Mother Alice would walk the two miles down
from Skyland and knock at our door. She and Mama would
have tea and sandwiches in the front parlor. After they had
finished their visit, Mama would drive her back up the hill to
Skyland.

Clara remembered once when Mother Alice came to
visit shortly after Brother was born in 1916. Mrs.
Benninghoven remarked on what beautiful eyes the baby
had. Brother was sound asleep.

If I should happen to come home and find Mama
entertaining this strange woman in the long white sheets, I
would be very startled and try to get away as quickly as
possible. Mrs. Benninghoven was tall and gaunt, like a
skeleton in sheets. She had an ageless face. She could have
been two thousand years old. She frightened me, just as if
one of the drawings from my Sunday school books had
materialized in our parlor. She even spoke in biblical phrases,
using thee, thou and ye.

Emma Mae wrote this description of Mother Alice for
a school paper:

"Mother Alice, as she called herself, stood near the
counter of a little country store, purchasing a dimes worth of

garlic. A yellow braided straw bag hung over her left arm. She wore a pair of dusty sandals over her bare feet, and a loose fitting attire, made from a sheet, was draped around her tall figure. A yellow piece of gauze was coiled around her head in the form of a turban representing the 'Hindoo' head dress. The hollow piercing beady eyes were nearly hidden by her turban, but her long pointed nose was a prominent part of her face. Her thin drawn lips were clinched to-gether over her sunken toothless mouth, and a ghastly appearance of desperate trouble was marked on her stiff pallid wrinkles."

Once, Mother Alice showed Mama and me a picture of herself when she was young. She had been very beautiful.[53]

A QUARTER OF A MILE down the road from Mother Alice, lived Mrs. Spranger. She was a contemporary of Mother Alice, and was also very tall and gaunt. She was known as a wealthy old miser, who was rumored to have money hidden under her mattress. I know she kept money hidden, because she paid me for some housework with this money, and it was yellowed with age.

Mrs. Spranger was one of the heirs to the Crocker Bank fortune. I worked for her the summer I was seventeen. She was about ninety years old then, and she hired me to clean house for three dollars an hour. I didn't want to work for her at all, so I asked that exorbitant wage! My sister Emma Mae was shocked when she heard how much I was getting. She said, "But Margaret, a registered nurse only gets three dollars an hour." This was in 1944.

Mrs. Spranger hired me for only two hours a day. She mostly wanted me to fetch her mail and fix her lunch, but she saw to it that I worked the whole time. She wanted to make sure she got her money's worth. So she had me dust rooms that hadn't been dusted in thirty years. I developed an allergic reaction to the dust. That's when I discovered that

[53] Mother Alice wrote two books: *Born of the Spirit*, and *A Martyr's Vision*. She was born in 1863 in Maine. She moved to Skyland in 1901, and lived there until her death in 1944. (Ed.)

money isn't everything.

Mama said forty years prior to this, Mrs. Spranger had been married. She kept such tight control over her money, loving it above all else, that her husband took off in a cloud of dust. She spent a small fortune hiring detectives to follow him all over the world. (Of course, if she hadn't been so stingy in the first place, this might never have happened.)

He never returned, and she lived the rest of her life alone.

Mr. Wagner lived a mile from Mrs. Spranger, and she would walk down the hill to visit him about once a year. He was a reclusive man, and didn't have contact with many other people in the mountains. He never went out into the community. We often wondered how he got his food and other essentials. His lights were always on every time we drove past his house, even if it was four o'clock in the morning.

THEN THERE WAS WHISPERING DAVE. He had lived in the mountains long before my time, but Mama would mention him every so often. He had been kicked in the throat by a horse when he was a young man. After that, he could only speak in a hoarse whisper.

Kids being kids, they would stand outside of his house at night and howl until they got his dogs barking. Whispering Dave would go to his window, throw it open, and whisper as loud as he could, "Shut up!"

The kids would stop just long enough to let the dogs quiet down, then they would start them up all over again.

MAMA TOLD US ABOUT JIM DAVIS, who was also before my time. Jim had lived near the Rapps in Missouri, but the family had never liked him. His wife had died mysteriously of a sudden illness. Some of the neighbors suspected foul play, but nothing was ever proven. Jim moved to the Santa Cruz Mountains about the same time as the Rapp family.

He had the peculiar habit of falling in love with every available woman in the mountains. (Most were not available.) If they didn't return his affection, he would threaten to take Ruff on Rats. This was a powerful rodent killer laced with strychnine.

Aunt Rena was once the target of his misguided affections. She was about twenty-five at the time. She was a quiet, nervous woman who would go hide in the back of the house whenever she heard him coming. He would start bawling, "Rena! Rena, where are you? I love you, Rena! If you don't come out, honey, I'm going to take Ruff on Rats!" He would keep this up for two or three hours, or until one of her brothers—usually Papa—would come along and chase him away with his gun.

Mama was also once the object of his desire. She was a naive sixteen year old at the time. She accepted a ride in his buggy. She was coming from the Burrell store, and this would have been a slow ride up the hill to Skyland. Her father rode up on horse back and told Mama to get out of the buggy.

Emma Mae told me that Jim Davis later married a very nice woman. She was a piano teacher, and they lived on the Hoops Place. Emma Mae and Elizabeth used to walk over and take piano lessons from her.

THE REVEREND GEORGE GODSMAN (I swear that was his real name!) lived with his old battle axe wife (that's what *he* called her) and his unmarried stepson, Clarence Martini. Clarence was in his sixties by this time, and the Reverend and his wife were in their eighties.

Mrs. Godsman always wore a hat with a black net veil pulled down under her chin and tied in the back of her neck. The lace was covered with solid black dots, so you never saw her face. I never saw her without the veil. I always wondered what she was hiding from, and had no idea what she looked like. My brother Frank said she kissed him once through her black veil. That must have been a frightening experience for a small child.

Mama was a Presbyterian and had been attending Skyland Church for most of her life. However, after Reverend Godsman arrived, her attendance dropped off, as she was not particularly fond of his sermons. She was also in the middle of the discord in the Harmony Missionary Society, of which Mrs. Godsman was on the other side. I seldom attended the Skyland Church, as I had converted to Catholicism when I was nine.

When I was ten years old, Mama thought it would be nice if we went to church together for Mother's Day service. She thought it would be spiritually uplifting for both of us. We arrived early and got a front pew. The Reverend began his sermon by throwing a chair up in the air! He said, "What goes up, must come down," proving that gravity was indeed a fact. (The Reverend Godsman was a firm believer in the law of gravity.)

This display warmed him up to his main topic of the day, which was alcoholism. He solicited the help of his stepson, Clarence Martini, to aid him in the alcohol demonstration. (At that time I had no idea what a martini was, so the irony of his name escaped me.)

Clarence started out by asking if any of the young gentlemen in the congregation thought they could break an egg by squeezing the two ends together, very tightly. Evidently this is usually difficult to do; but the egg slipped and broke, with most of the egg spilling onto the floor. Clarence, who already had the alcohol in the frying pan, leapt through the air and caught a small amount of the egg in the frying pan—just in the nick of time!

Holy cow! Even with a small amount of egg, I could actually hear the sizzling, frying sound of egg in the alcohol. The Reverend pointed out that this is what happens to the brain when you drink alcohol![54]

I was impressed! I sneaked a sideways glance at Mama. She had that set look on her face which she got when she was not amused. She definitely was not impressed by this little demonstration.

The Reverend then asked the entire congregation to stand and take the oath of abstinence from alcohol, swearing

---

[54] In recent years, this demonstration has been copied on national television with regards to drug abuse. However the original conception, brought to the mountains by Reverend Godsman and Clarence Martini in regards to alcoholism, was much more entertaining. (Au. & Ed.)

that we would never touch a drop of the stuff for the rest of our lives. I stood, along with the rest of the congregation. We were all swept up in the emotion of the moment. But what was this? Oh, how embarrassing. Mama was not standing, nor did she repeat the oath. I was mortified to think that Mama would defy a man of the cloth!

Mama, who was not given to much alcohol consumption, thought she might still like to keep her options open.

The last time I heard one of Reverend Godsman's sermons, he was eighty-three years old. His wife had just died, and he was leaving the mountains to live with a daughter of his in Sacramento. This was his final sermon, and the whole family went in tribute to Mrs. Godsman. (Even though Mama and she had not always been on the best terms, Mama did not carry a grudge into the next world.)

The Reverend commenced his sermon by throwing a chair up into the air once again, this time in a spirit of celebration. He cried out, "I'm free!"

BEST FRIENDS

DELPHINE PARKER and Mama were best friends, almost from the first moment they met in 1925. Mama called her friend "Phinie." Mrs. Parker was high strung, spoke rather fast, and was always bickering with her husband John, calling him her worse half. In fact, in one letter she wrote Mama in November of 1934, she ended it with: "I must ring off as my worse half wants his dinner."

She was also a charming woman. She loved children, and was full of fun and mischievousness herself. When I think about her now, I think of happiness and beauty and sunshine and flowers. Mrs. Parker surrounded herself with beautiful possessions. She was wealthy during the depression, when almost everyone else I knew was short of money.

When I heard that Mrs. Parker had come to the mountains for one of her stays, I would walk a mile or so out of my way just to "happen" by her cottage. When she answered the door, I would stand there speechless, so she carried on a one sided conversation with me. "Margaret dear, how are you? It's so lovely to see you." I would hang my head and look at my bare feet. "Would you like a piece of candy, dear?" This was what I had walked that extra mile for. How had she guessed? Candy was something I otherwise got once a year, when we paid our grocery bill. I would look up just long enough to bob my head in agreement. She would step back into her cottage and bring me out a handful of gaily wrapped chocolate-filled hard candies, which she put into my small eager hands. She usually had another little gift for me which she had brought down from Capwell's department store in Oakland, where she lived. She would say, "Oh yes, Margaret, I have brought you a delightful book all about birds." She would then show me a most beautiful book with lots of colored pictures.

This practice went on from the time I was five or six until I was about twelve. I would like to be able to say that I smiled politely and said, "thank you." But my social graces were not yet developed. I would run off, opening my candies as I ran, devouring them along the way. I did love Mrs. Parker, and I'm sure she felt this, and that she understood. She had been poor during her childhood.

Mrs. Parker did stand out as being from another world, i.e. another class. She and the Captain, as we referred to her husband John Parker, had lived in Honolulu for many years. He had been the engineer in charge of dredging out Pearl Harbor, and also Lake Merritt in Oakland. They had three children: Esmond, John, and Anne. Esmond and John remained in Honolulu and were in charge of the entertainment for the island, while Captain Parker, Mrs. Parker, and their daughter Anne returned to the mainland. The Parkers invested most of their money in apartment buildings in Oakland. During the twenties and thirties, Oakland was considered a very nice city to live in.

One day the Captain was reading the *Oakland Tribune* and saw an advertisement for The Willows, a resort in the Santa Cruz Mountains. Mrs. Parker was opposed to purchasing The Willows. She thought the Santa Cruz Mountains were in the boondocks. She had never been there and had no idea of their tremendous beauty. The Captain and Delphine were always sputtering at each other. The cartoon characters "The Lockhorns" remind me of their relationship. The Captain won this round, and he purchased The Willows. However, Mrs. Parker fell in love with the mountains as soon as she saw them. She spent much of her time up there—as much as she could get away with. Mr. Parker rarely came with her, and I'm sure he quickly regretted his decision to buy the place.

The Willows had been a thriving resort. It had a huge indoor swimming pool with many dressing rooms. There were exotic plants from all over the world. There was also another natural pool in a redwood grove which was fed by a live stream and the overflow created a waterfall.

This grove was where Mrs. Parker gave me my sixth birthday party. She put up lots of balloons, streamers and had carnival games and imported about twenty children from Oakland. It was a very unusual children's party for the mountains. There were only three or four children about my age who lived within a couple of miles of our place.

There was also a large English-style country house at The Willows. It was u-shaped, with many bedrooms leading out into a central courtyard. Unfortunately, this house later burned to the ground, as did the cottage in which her daughter Anne used to spend her summer vacations.

The Parkers entertained many interesting guests at The Willows. Max Baer, the heavyweight champion, was the most famous one I remember. Mrs. Parker was also friends with author Jack London, who, like the Parkers, lived in Oakland and spent a great deal of time in the Santa Cruz Mountains.[55]

There were several cottages and smaller cabins on the property, which had been rented out when The Willows was operated as a resort. Grandpa Ingraham saw that the Parkers weren't planning on renting these cabins. He suggested to Mrs. Parker that she let the poor and homeless move into them. Grandpa had been an orphan and he couldn't bear to see waste or poverty. Mrs. Parker said, "I was poor too, Hiram, and I don't plan to be poor again."

The Parkers were of English descent. The Captain

---

[55] Jack London, and other literary figures of the day, hung out at a little hotel which earned the nickname "Bungalow Bohemia," as it was part of an artist colony that sprang up in the neighborhood of Whitewash Alley. This was even farther out than Burrell, where Loma Prieta Road begins to head up the mountain. It was just past the site of a new café called The Highland Trading Post. Whitewash Alley got its name because of a row of perfectly whitewashed picket fences that adorned the houses along Loma Prieta Road.

This little "Bohemia" held an attraction for the literary community in the last part of the nineteenth century because one of their own lived on Whitewash Alley: Josephine Clifford McCrackin. Besides London, other notable writers of the day vacationed there, including: Ambrose Bierce, George Sterling, Herman Scheffauer, and—the best known of all—Mark Twain. (Ed.)

was born in England, and Mrs. Parker was born in the United States of English parents. The Captain seemed particularly British. He would sit behind his newspaper with the smoke from his cigar billowing over the top of it. I thoroughly expected to see the newspaper catch on fire one day—there was so much smoke. If Delphine said anything to him, he would harumph and mumble and growl.

Mrs. Parker was an excellent cook. I remember going with her and Mama on many picnics, usually to the beach. She would bring dainty little cucumber sandwiches and delicate looking *petit fours*. Whenever Mama and I would visit her in her home she always served us a delicious meal, followed by tea poured from her hand painted tea pot with pink rose buds, which was always covered with a cozy to keep it warm. She would bring out her cookie jar, which was equally exquisite, filled with luscious cookies. I got my love of beautiful dishes from Mrs. Parker, as well as my love of sweets.

I got over my fear of answering the telephone when Mama tried to call me once to invite me over to eat with them. I stood by the phone, afraid to lift the receiver. When I found out what I had missed, I never let that happen again!

Mrs. Parker baked delicious cakes for the Harmony Missionary Society meetings, a charitable organization in the mountains which Mama and she belonged to. Her attitude towards charitable contributions was expressed in this letter of November, 1934: "Mrs. Orchison and I are going to get a quilt from the cotton mills and send it to North Fork. I would rather send as much as we can to the home missions. Mrs. Wragg wants most of her money to go to foreign missions, but we have so many in our own country that needs help just now. It is better to send what we can to our own."

After the Parkers sold the bulk of their property at The Willows to the Enloes in 1934, the Parkers retained enough land to build a small cottage. Mrs. Parker began working on her husband to do this about a year in advance of the sale. "I think I am exhausted trying to talk my husband into building me a little place up there," Mrs. Parker wrote in April of 1933. "He might as well do it first as last as I won't stop talking about it until he does."

Mrs. Parker continued making her frequent jaunts to the mountains after the cottage was built. The Captain came less and less often.

Mrs. Parker loved flowers and she always had an English-style garden. I remember her delphiniums, snapdragons, and hollyhocks in particular. She was always fighting the gophers and the water shortage. She always had a beautiful garden, even with these obstacles.

Mrs. Parker was never comfortable driving in the mountains. The roads were really bad in those days. Besides being winding and narrow, the unpaved roads were dusty in summer and muddy with deep ruts in winter. Mama felt sorry for her dear friend and would often catch a ride to Los Gatos so she could drive Phinie up the mountain road. When Mrs. Parker had to go back to Oakland, Mama would often drive her to Los Gatos and hope to catch a ride back up to the mountains. Mama was usually lucky, and would see someone in town who could drive her back. Los Gatos was so small in those days, with a population of about four thousand, so Mama could always spot a familiar face. Everyone thought Mama was a little crazy to do this for Delphine, but that didn't matter to her.

Mrs. Parker's attitude about Mama's generosity in doing this was expressed in a letter from March, 1937, in which she writes: "Dearest, Was so glad you found a way to get home. I felt rather guilty taking you to Los Gatos and dropping you off, not knowing how you would get back. I almost turned and went back to take you home, so I was delighted to hear how nicely you got home. My conscience was at peace."

These two women came from different social worlds, yet in many ways they were very much alike. They were both kind and generous, and both had a keen sense of humor. Both of them could also speak their minds with any provocation. They would not let anyone walk all over them. However, I never heard of them having a dispute with each other.

Mrs. Parker was a very articulate, cultured and witty person. Since her letters are so entertaining, I have included

a few of the best examples from her extensive correspondence with Mama below:

Nov. 1, 1935

Dear Friend,
Well, here I am back in my apartment. It seems real
good to be back where it is nice and warm. I just got out in
time as it is raining quite hard.
I had quite a little trouble getting out of that road. It
was quite damp and skiddy and my car was cold and kept
stopping on the hill so I got tired of trying to get it up and
asked Mr. Enloe to help. I lost about twenty-five minutes but
it worked out all right as I picked up Margaret and Philip and
some boys near the bridge and some other children near the
highway for the Summit school. By the bridge was covered
with ice.
I arrived home in good time, 2 1/2 hours. John was
quite surprised to see me walk in. He made me some hot
coffee and that warmed me up.
I rented my cottage yesterday to a man. He writes
books. He has a lot of whiskers on his face, so I told John I
rented the cottage to a fuller brush man and when he saw him,
he said, "I hear you are a fuller brush man." I felt so silly, but
an Englishman can't see a joke.
My they are having such awful earthquakes in Mon-
tana. No let up to them.
Well, dear, I just wanted you to know I arrived home
OK.

Much love from me.

Mrs. Parker mentions Frankie and Mrs. R. in the next
letter. She and Mama didn't think too much of the Roosevelts,
as evidenced by this letter:

Feb. 13, 1938

Dear Friend,
Received your letter and was glad to hear you hadn't

turned into a mermaid. Still, it might have been nice in a way. I might have met up with you at Waikiki and had a nice swim together. Well, who knows. I nearly met up with you in South Dakota last year. Well maybe that's too good to be true.

I can't get my shopping done as I have a cold and don't want it to get worse, so I'll stay in and keep warm.

I see Anemometer, the Weather Bureau cat, was starting out in the rain, the weather man asked him where in the mischief he was going. He said to see Noah. He had to find out right away how to build an ark. So it might be well if someone found out how to build one.

John was saying he thought we ought to go to Europe. I told him I thought Calif. was bad enough.

One thing we ought to have water enough to last all year. I do think it will do the fruit trees a world of good. But of course, we don't want too much fruit or our dear Frankie will make us burn it up.

Don't you think Mrs. R. looks like a fool with her hair cut? Her teeth stick out like the quills on a fretful porcupine. She was ugly enough before.

We expect to leave now on the 23 of this month. First it was 12, then 18, now 23. So I thought sure I would get up to the Mts. once more before we left. But it doesn't look like it now. I will write you once more before I go.

Loads of Love, Me

She and the captain were in Hawaii when she sent Mama this next letter:

April 6, 1938

Dear Friend,

Received your ever welcome letter. And was very pleased, indeed, to hear you haven't been drowned yet. It's about time we have some nice weather. It's a miserable day here today, raining and blowing a gale. There was a crowd of us going over to the other side of the Island and cook steaks over charcoal but no can do in this rain.

I am having such a good time, I don't think I'll ever

settle down again.

It certainly was too bad about Mr. Morrell committing suicide. He might have found some other way out. I can't understand how he could have a mortgage on his place. It seems to me, in all the years he has owned it, he ought to have it paid off by now. It's strange how some people never pay for anything. If they want a little money, the first thing they do is mortgage their home or farm. It's not always so easy to pay it off. It will make it bad for his wife.[56]

I am glad you got to the Missionary meeting at Mrs. Woods, but very sorry you had to walk. That's where you miss your side kick. It's strange how they all hate to do any work for the Circle, but oh boy, how they love to go. Mrs. H. had her gall to want to be vice president when she knew you were always vice president with me.

I hope they have the roads in good condition by the time I get back so we can sally forth on some of our jaunts.

Oceans of Love, D.P.

---

[56] We were unable to confirm this story in contemporary local press accounts. A Mr. Morrell was not listed in Santa Cruz County death records for the first quarter of 1938 either. However, he would most likely have been a relation of the pioneering Morrell brothers from the Summit area, as both of the brothers had died by this time. He could very likely have died in another county, but still held property in the mountains. In her letter, Mrs. Parker sounds as if she is responding to some news in a letter from Mama; however, this is conjecture. (Ed.)

CLARA REMEMBERS THE
ROARING '20S

I ASKED MY SISTER CLARA to tell me about the roaring twenties. Although she was only fourteen when the stock market crashed in 1929, she had a keen memory and remembered many stories from those exciting days. Here are some of the things she told me about:

"How I hated the song, 'There's Music in the Air.' I was six, Elizabeth was twelve, and Emma Mae was ten.[57] They walked faster than I did, and I was little. They would get ahead on the way to school. When we got to the Clough's, near Skyland, I'd start crying. They would sing, 'There's Music in the Air.' At school, the teacher would ask the children what we'd like to sing. Emma Mae and Elizabeth would pipe up, 'There's music in the Air.'

"Then came the roaring twenties. Women got the vote. Then came prohibition, bootlegging, bath tub gin, speakeasies, the flappers, and a new dance—the Charleston. You could cut a rug to the tune of "Yes, We have no Bananas," "Ain't She Sweet, Coming Down the Street...," "Sleepy Time Gal," "Tea for Two," "Nola," and others. They danced the Paul Jones, Virginia Reel, Fox Trot, Waltz, and so on. People drank bath tub gin and died. The more brazen swains (beaus) took their flames to speakeasies where they would be admitted if they knew the right password. They were often raided and liquor was poured down the street, and people were jailed. But if they weren't, they sparked (smooched) all the way home.

"Mr. Meyer had the biggest still in the mountains. For

---

[57] This was in 1921. (Ed.)

the benefit of the Feds, [he said] he just made liquor for medicinal purposes. This was permissible.

"During prohibition, it was even against the law for a housewife to let a jar of fruit juice ferment. She was liable to go to jail. It was illegal for a man to take some brandy to an unfortunate citizen who was unconscious, or to take a bottle of beer from your house and take it to another.

"You couldn't buy cigarettes on Sundays.

"The flappers painted their faces usually with a tiny black spot high on their cheek, wore lots of mascara, and wore long waisted short (to their knees) dresses. Slacks or pants for women were still unheard of. But bobbing your hair began. The bobbed hair was originated by Irene Castle, a famous dancer. She singed her hair getting a marcel with a hot iron, and had to cut it very short. It looked nice on her, and the bob became the latest hair style.

"I remember Emma Mae and Elizabeth coming home from Mrs. Miller's with their hair bobbed and shocking Mama and Papa. When they bought knickers from the catalog, the folks thought sure their daughters were going to the dogs. Any girl dressed like that was asking for it, Mama said. Knickers were wide hipped pants, tapered at the knee and buttoned just below the knees.

"Now if you were too old to cut the mustard, you could play cards such as pedro or whist. Mama thought poker was sinful. That was gambling.

"Mama liked a good time as well as the next one. It was said that an Ingraham would get up out of the grave to go somewhere. However, it had to be according to all moral codes. It was all right to have girls and boys at a party, but they were not to pair up. One time she walked into the parlor and the girls were either on the arm of the young bucks, or on their laps. Mama just calmly said, 'Everyone take your own seats.'

"If the hour was getting late, say after midnight, and the swains were still in the parlor, Papa would simply turn off the Delco light generator. A gentler hint to get them to go home."

Clara did not describe what went on in the parlor

crammed full of girls and swains after the lights to the whole house were shut off.

"In 1922, Papa bought a Maxwell, a touring car with a running board. It was enclosed with leather sides with rising windows that snapped on the doors, that were made of soft, clear plastic. Now we could go to San Jose in one day, not like with the horse and buggy! When we took the buggy, we had to stay over night in a hotel.

"Mama would get us to Santa Cruz for our annual camping trip under any adversity. We usually went over the Fourth of July. That was a slow time on the ranch, before the pears and prunes had to be harvested. One year she had poison oak so bad she could hardly crawl, but she took us anyway. Then she soaked in the salt water in the ocean. It burned her skin, but she believed that if it hurt it was a good cure.

"We always had the running boards on the Maxwell lined up with cousins and other neighbor children. She could never refuse anyone a ride. It's a wonder there were no accidents. But then no one drove very fast.

"Before the Maxwell, we went to Santa Cruz on the spring wagon. Of course Papa drove the horse. He took hay for them. Mama and Papa slept in style in the tent. The children slept on the wagon in the hay. We stayed until the horses ate up our bed, and then we went home.

"Our trips to San Jose were always adventurous. Once, there was a circus in town, so Papa said we had to go. We ate at the Coffee Club in San Jose, and Mama grew faint. She went to the rest room, which was actually a rest room because they had cots, and laid down. But first she took off her glasses and laid them down on the wash basin. After her fainting spell, she got up to get her glasses and they were gone! Mama couldn't see a thing without her glasses. She borrowed Papa's, but they were the wrong prescription. Somehow, Mama drove us to the circus without causing an accident.

"We were late getting to the circus, and when we went into the big tent, the parade was just behind us. The el-

Three cousins in a basket — Frank Rapp, Phyllis Griner and Bob Hurney in 1922.

ephants, the clowns, the cages with the lions, everything followed us in. Mama was running to keep ahead of them, and the children of all different sizes were running along, the older ones carrying the babies. Papa had long legs so he just walked fast. People were laughing, evidently thinking we were part of the show. Just then Aunt Lydia yelled out from the audience, 'Hey Emma, what in the *@#* are you doing in the parade?' Mama was mortified.

"In order to get a license to drive in the twenties, all you had to do was go to the Department of Vehicles and declare that you knew how to drive, or have a friend say you can drive. Farm boys were allowed to drive when they got to be fourteen.

"Once Mama made a 'Hollywood' stop, which meant she didn't come to a complete stop at an intersection. Officer Feathers, who later became the chief of police, pulled her over. He looked inside the car and saw all of the children, the Hurney cousins were with us. He let Mama go with a lecture of how she should come to a complete stop.

"Papa believed in progress. He had the first Delco light battery, the first Imperial prunes, and the first radio in the mountains. Mr. Hart, who wired the house for electricity and put in the Delco lights, made Papa the radio. Papa gave him eighteen dollars a piece for the tubes, and he made the radio. I believe there were three tubes. There was no speaker, just ear phones. Brother and I used to share them. He listened with one side and I listened with the other.

"There wasn't much to listen to or many stations. KQW in San Jose was the main one. Mostly there was farm news, some music, jokes and riddles. In later years, we got KPO, KGO, KFRC (from San Francisco.) Sometimes if the voices could go through the air pockets we got KHJ from Los Angeles, which stood for Kindness, Hope and Joy. Our favorite show was "Amos and Andy."

"Radio listening was encouraged. Our teacher Mrs. Eggleston was great on music appreciation. Radios were getting more prevalent and the programs were more varied. At ten in the morning, the children all went to the nearest neighbor who had a radio and listened to "The Standard Oil

Hour," which lasted about fifteen minutes. They explained all of the instruments and how they make symphony music. Then at eight in the evening, we were supposed to listen to the whole hour of music. I especially remember the William Tell Overture.

"Of course there was the victorola, a 1905 model with cylinder tubes that you had to wind up. John McCormick and the Two Black Crows was my favorite act. I thought they were hilarious when one Black Crow said, 'I'll meet you by the fence. If you get there first, draw a white line. And if I get there first, I'll rub it out.'

"Some of the movies I remember from that time were: 'Covered Wagon,' 'Ben Hur,' 'Ramona,' and 'Seventh Heaven,' which we saw at Holy City. At Holy City movies were shown on Saturday nights, with a chapter of a serial so you would come back the next week. The format was the main feature, a short comedy skit (about twenty minutes), and then a travelogue.

"The larger movie houses had a vaudeville skit. Piano or organ music was played for mood effects. The first talking picture I saw was Al Jolson in 'Sonny Boy,' and when he sang 'Mammy' going down on his knees, I cried. Eddie Cantor was coming into his own. Clara Bow was the 'It Girl.' She never made it in the talkies."

CHRISTMAS was always a big deal in our family. Since I grew up during the depression, I remember it a little differently, though. Clara gives a really good impression of what Christmas was like in the twenties:

"I was about six when I found out about Santa Claus. I was going through my mother's dresser drawers when I found the little china dishes Santa was going to bring me. They were made in Germany. Of course Mama assured me there was a Santa Claus, and I was not supposed to tell Brother or Mary about my find.

"Mama made a lot over Christmas. We would go out into the forest with Papa the day before Christmas, chop the tree, and set it up by the dining room steps. That night Santa would trim the tree. When we got up in the morning we saw the most dazzling and glittering tree with all the toys and presents.

"Aunt May and Uncle Louis, Grandma and Grandpa, Uncle Will Baars and Aunt Kate, and Mr. [Henry] Garner were all usually there for Christmas dinner. Uncle Will played Santa, although at the time we didn't know it. I remember giving him some cider and he choked on it.

"One Christmas there wasn't much under the tree, but Santa left a note that he had an accident with his sleigh and would be back, probably about New Year. Sure enough, on New Year's Eve we were in the parlor and heard noises. Then the sliding doors closed, and Santa was on the other side, in the dining room where the tree was. Then he left and the doors opened. And there were all of our dolls and toys.

"Yes, Mama made a big thing out of Christmas. I guess that's why I have, and have carried it on to my daughter Audrey. I heard it said once that Mama had said, "If Clara starves to death, she'll have a Christmas.""

CLARA SHED LIGHT on the courtship between one of the hired hands on the ranch and one of our sisters. Since Clara was still a kid when this was going on, she observed things that the older folks were slow to pick up on.

"Jack Callaghan worked on the ranch for Papa for room and board, tobacco money, and twenty-five dollars a month. Later he got a pay raise, and Papa upped it to thirty dollars a month.

"Elizabeth and Emma Mae were away at high school by this time. They came home on weekends and went back on Sunday afternoon. Jack got a car and began taking them back and forth. When he took them back on Sunday, Jack would take them both to a movie. Then he left Elizabeth off first, then Emma Mae. People began to suspect he was courting one of them, but couldn't figure out which one.

"It was apparent to me. When we picked prunes, I noticed after Jack hauled a load of prunes by horse and sled to the dry yard and brought back empty boxes to fill, he would then go to sit under Elizabeth's tree, seemingly to help her. I always liked to fill my own boxes. Elizabeth, knowing

A stylish family in 1926 — Ernest and Belle Griner, pictured with their first two girls, Phyllis (r.) and Virginia.

it would make me mad, told Jack to dump a pail of prunes into my box. She got the desired effect. I took the prunes and dumped them on his head, screaming, 'I'm going to get my father to fire you!'

"Until the day Jack died, he'd tease me, saying 'You don't look like the girl in the prune orchard.' Jack was like a brother to us. Another incident occurred when we were harvesting grapes. I am not sure what Jack's job was, but it could have been picking grapes and making crates. Elizabeth was packing. (Papa had red, white and blue grapes, and had them packed in red, white and blue stripes. We used to win prizes with these grapes.) Everyone had an hour off at noon. I noticed Jack went into the packing house early and, soon after, Elizabeth followed. Of course nosey Clara had to go and see what was happening. I arrived just as they were smooching. They naturally told me that I hadn't seen a thing.

"Jack asked Papa for Elizabeth's hand, and Papa gave it. They were married November 30, 1929, just before Advent. In those days, Catholics couldn't get married during Advent.

"IN 1929 CAME THE CRASH! Stock markets and banks closed. Papa received about ten percent of his money. The bank manager, Mr. Hamsher, went broke trying to pay some of the clients with his own money.

"Then there were ten years of depression. People had no jobs. They were selling apples on the street for a dime. The WPA began, and the farmers were paid for not raising crops. Papa didn't accept this. Papa's health broke, and he received thirty dollars a month from his insurance. We called our outside toilet 'Frankie's toilet' as it was built by the WPA while Franklin D. Roosevelt was in office. My folks were Republican, and really didn't believe in governmental interference.

"For lack of something to do, there was marathon dancing until the couples fell on the floor. And there was flag pole sitting. One incident I remember most, a young couple tried to see how long they could dance on a small platform on a thirty foot flagpole atop a four story department store building. I forgot how many days they danced before they finally stopped. I went to see them three or four times.

"I remember going to San Jose with Mama, Papa and Jack to watch the election returns flashed on a building downtown. That was the Hoover disaster, and Franklin D. Roosevelt had won the [1932] election. Jack and Papa watched the returns, and Mama and I went to a talking movie."

CLEMENT BRAKE

CLARA WENT ON TO TELL the following story about a Laurel boy who made good:

"Mama thought the sun rose and set on Clement Brake. He was just a boy in his early teens when he was staying with his mother in her summer home in Laurel. His family was in the retail business in San Jose.

"Clement asked Mr. Napier, who owned the store at Laurel, if he knew of anyone who needed a boy to work on a farm. Mr. Napier asked Papa if he could use a young man to help on the ranch. Papa said he could.

"Clement stayed in the windmill house on the Blabon Place, a one-roomed building with a windmill on the top. One day he came in and Elizabeth and Emma Mae were playing with something under the bed. He asked, 'What do you have there?' Elizabeth said, 'a goder snake.' Elizabeth was four and Emma Mae was two. Clement looked, and to his amazement, it was a rattler with six rattles. Needless to say, he killed it.

"Another time he heard Mama screaming at the back of the place. He ran to see what was the matter. And there in front of her was a rattle snake coiled, ready to strike. However he got there in time, and it struck at him, getting its fangs into his pants leg. He grabbed a big stick and killed the snake. He took twelve rattles out of that one. (The more rattles, the older the snake.)

"The first summer he worked for Papa, Clement emphatically refused to come in the house and eat. He wanted to make it on his own. That was the summer of 1913, and he was a lad of fourteen. The next summer, Mama said, 'Adolph, I won't let you hire Clement unless you insist that he comes in the house to eat.'

178

"Clement came to help pick prunes, or whatever there was to do, the summers of 1913, 1914 and 1915, the summer I was born. Clement made such an impression on Papa that he said to Mama, 'That boy is going to make something of himself.' And so he did.

"After he served in the Navy during World War I, Clement went into the retail business with his uncle. Later he managed Capwell's in Oakland for six years. When he was on buying trips in New York or Paris, he would send toys to Emma Mae and Elizabeth, some of which they still have.

"Through the years he always kept in touch with Mama and Papa. There were sometimes years in between visits. When he came, he would try and fool Papa and pretend to be a buyer for his fruit. He would ask the usual questions, such as the approximate tonnage for his pears or prunes. Then after offering Papa a price, he would cough or smile, and Papa would say, 'Oh, Clement!'

"Clement loved to come up and fish with Papa in Soquel Creek.

"In 1936, while I was recuperating from pneumonia, Clement visited them and mentioned that Vallejo wasn't feeling the depression as much as the other areas because of the Mare Island Ship Yard. That's when I got the idea to go to Vallejo and start a beauty shop, along with my sister Mary. We began our business in October, 1939.

"When I contracted polio in 1945, Mama went to see Clement. After she told him about me, he sat down and cried with her."

CLARA, WHO PROVIDED THE STORIES for these two chapters, should have a book written about her. She did write her own book, an endeavor which she said Clement encouraged her in. It was called *From Soap to Nuts*,[58] and was a collection of old family recipes.

Clara was always fun loving and generous. When she was twenty-five, she married Gorm Christian Clausen.

---

[58] "Soap" is not a typo for "Soup." The book included a recipe to make homemade soap. (Ed.)

Unfortunately, when Clara was twenty-nine, she got polio during the epidemic. She was so sick she almost died. She was very sick for a year, and did not sit up and put her feet over the bed until November, 1946.

Clara had a little girl named Audrey, who was terrified of having a fire in the fireplace as they lived upstairs. If the house caught on fire, how would her mother escape in her wheelchair? But Brother cut out a square in the corner of Clara's bedroom and installed an elevator. This operated up until the time she died, almost fifty years!

Clara was very politically active in promoting passage of legislation to help people confined in wheelchairs, such as getting ramps installed in public places, creating special stalls in public bathrooms, and paving sloped curbs. She was president of the indoor sports club, and they worked together on fundraising drives and wrote letters to the state legislature.

Clara also continued to run her business after her illness, and was even named queen of cosmetology at a San Francisco convention one year. She kept active, and never let the unfortunate consequences of her bout with polio get her down.

THE BUCKET BRIGADE

THERE WAS NO FIRE DEPARTMENT in the early days of the Santa Cruz Mountains. The fire department in town couldn't hope to get there in time. And of course, there were fires!

In the case of fire, the mountain communities would be alerted by a continuous ringing of the church bell. Also, the operator at Central, Mrs. Sharp, would open all of the lines and ring five long rings. When she heard the clicks of everyone picking up their receivers, she would announce where the fire was.

During fire season, a lookout station on top of Loma Prieta Mountain was manned twenty-four hours a day by Mrs. Sharp's husband. If he spotted a fire, he called Central.

Everyone sprung into action as soon as the alarm sounded. Every man, woman and child would arrive at the fire with a bucket in hand. Despite their good intentions, this was not the most efficient way to fight a fire. I don't remember hearing about a single house, cottage or barn that was saved in this way. By the time the volunteers on the bucket brigade had arrived, the important thing was to contain the fire, and make sure that no one was hurt.

Fires were to be dreaded. The mountains, with their lush vegetation and dense forests, have always been prone to fires.

THERE WERE MANY FAMOUS FIRES around Skyland. One of the first that I remember hearing about was the Blabon Place cottage. It burned to the ground, but the fire was contained.

After the ashes had cooled, Clara was poking through the rubble when she found "The Waffle Iron." We used it for several years, heating it on the wood burning stove. It made the best waffles! Unlike modern electric waffle irons, this one had to be turned over so that each side would brown. It had an ingenious ball and socket mechanism to rotate the iron without burning yourself. Then the handle fit back into the stand that raised it above the stove. This way the waffles didn't burn, but were a perfect golden brown. It was made of cast iron. Perhaps that's why it cooked the waffles so well.

My cousin Janet would ask, as soon as she got to the mountains, "Where is The Waffle Iron?" The first thing she wanted to do after arriving was make waffles.[59]

A COUPLE OF YEARS after the Blabon Place burned to the ground, Papa's barn burned to the ground. Papa was in Compton, in Southern California, at the time. He had gone with Jack, the hired hand who later married my sister Elizabeth. They went down to look at a piece of property that Salvadore was selling. Mama didn't go as someone had to look after the children and the farm.

Clara was eleven and she remembers clearly the barn burning. She was awakened about midnight by the familiar stomp, stomp, stomp, and Salvadore, clad in nothing but his drawers and his aluminum boots, calling out in his thunderous voice, "Fire! Fire!"

She looked out the window and saw a big wall of flame. His cabin, the shacks where the farm equipment was kept, and the barn were all on fire. The fact that Salvadore kept his dynamite in his cabin added to the excitement.

He lived in a two room cabin on the Crane Place. There was only one door, in the kitchen, where the fire started. He had a window in his bedroom through which he escaped.

Salvadore led the horses out of the barn, and to the back end of the property. By this time the neighbors had arrived. Steffi Fidel was first. They drove the car down to the redwoods to escape the fire.

---

[59] Immediately after that, Janet would go check out my dresser drawers to see what I had gotten since the previous summer— usually not much! (Au.)

The men formed a bucket brigade. They filled the buckets with water at the house and passed it up the line to the men on the rooftop of the packing house. Every time a spark or a flame shot up, a bucket of water was thrown on it. They worked fast, as it was a windy night.

Salvadore delighted in hopping from group to group with nothing on but his drawers and boots, shocking all of the women. He kept relating how he had flown through the window—like a bird!

He also kept bellowing, "Watch out, watch out!" because of the dynamite in the cabin.

When Papa returned from his trip, he built Salvadore a new cabin—with two doors—and a new barn for the horses.

This barn also burned down several years later. But by this time the plow horses, Molly and Dick, were gone. They had died and been replaced by a tractor. So there was no need to replace this barn. The site made a fertile place for Papa's garden.

Papa's garden became his delight. I have never tasted such delicious vegetables and berries as those he raised on that little plot that used to be where the barn was. He won many prizes at the Santa Cruz County Fair for his produce. We bought our first non-wood burning stove with the check for his cash prizes one year.

AUNT IDA'S OLD WOODEN two story house burned to the ground when I was six. Her son Bob, who was ten then, started the fire by adding gasoline to the wood stove to start the fire faster. It exploded and the house burned to the ground. Her son Floyd, who was seven then, reminded me that he came to live at our house for awhile.

The fire was truly awesome. I'll never forget my mixed feelings of excitement, fear, wonder and sadness—where were they going to live?

Although I'm sure it must have been hard for Aunt Ida, I enjoyed sleeping over with them while they were camping out in the barn that summer. I loved the smell of the fresh hay we slept on.

Uncle Will Hurney, Aunt Ida's husband, had bought their daughter a saxophone. She had no interest in learning to play, so Uncle Will took it up at age thirty-six. He became good enough to play at the Skyland dances, along with Charlotte Fidel, who played the piano, and Pete Delldot, who played the accordion.

The summer of the fire, Uncle Will was practicing and perfecting his technique. He liked to kid us and say that he had played the saxophone "over the radio." The radio was stored down in the horses stall with the rest of the furniture, and he was playing up in the loft where they slept.

ON AT LEAST TWO OCCASIONS, Mama prevented a major fire because of her keen sense of smell, and her quick action.

The first was when my sister Mary accidentally filled the kerosene lamps with gasoline. Mama came into the kitchen just as Mary was lighting the match. Mama said, "Drop that match, Mary!"

Mary stammered, "But I'm just lighting the..."

"You drop that match this instant!" Mama screamed. Mama almost never raised her voice to us, so Mary realized that Mama was serious. She dropped the match just in time to prevent a tragic explosion which could have maimed or killed her instantly.

The second occasion on which Mama prevented the house from burning down was one night when I was eleven. I wanted to finish a book I was reading. We were out of kerosene, so I lit a small candle. I stuck it on a piece of cardboard with a little wax from the candle. I went to bed and fell asleep while reading. It was a cold night so I had lots of blankets piled up. The candle burned down, burning through the cardboard. The sheets and the mattress began to smolder. Mama was just going down the Big Porch to her bedroom when she smelled the smoke. She came to my bedroom and jerked me out of bed. She hollered, "Quick! Help me carry the mattress out into the orchard!" I had been fast asleep and didn't know what she was talking about. I grumbled that I was asleep; it was cold; did we have to do it tonight? "Hurry up! Pick up the other end. Now!" Just as we got the mattress

Aunt Ida's barn, home to the family after their house burned to the ground. Only the second story is visible from the road. Photo taken in 1989. The barn still stands on Skyland Road in 1994.

out into the orchard, it burst into flames.

In 1964, my husband and children and I were living on Sheldon Avenue, in Santa Cruz. Mama called me up and said, "Your father and I are going to come and see you today, dear. We are starting in a few minutes."

I said that would be nice. About ten minutes later, Mama called back and said, "We aren't going to be able to come and see you today. The garage is on fire and my car is burning up." Mama had spotted the fire between the two phone calls. She ran out to try and get the car out of the garage. Doris Fidel had seen the fire from her place. She ran over to help. She got there just in time to see what Mama was doing. She screamed, "Emma, don't go in there!" Mama yelled back, "I'm going to get the car out!" Doris yelled back, "Don't go in there Emma, or I'll hit you over the head with this hoe!" Mama realized the sense in this and didn't go in.

The garage burned to the ground, and the car with it. Papa and his second cousin George Rapp and my son Larry rebuilt the garage. Larry was only fourteen at the time, but he was almost six feet tall, and he looked very grown up.

THEN THERE WAS A MYSTERIOUS fire in the redwood grove on our property when I was young. The perpetrators were never caught. There was a witness who didn't step forward at the time. He has long since passed on. The mystery has been smoldering for fifty-five years. Perhaps I can shed a little light on it.

There were two neighbor children younger than I was at the time, and I was about ten. We were having an exciting game of Cowboys and Indians. At an important moment in the game, Uncle Louis appeared coming up his road to the mailboxes in the redwood grove where we were playing. We had some lighted candles which we quickly disposed of in my parents mailbox, which adjoined Uncle Louis's. Later, we had a small campfire in the forest surrounding the road to our house. We found a bench between two redwood trees. The redwood trees had grown into the bench. It made a perfect campsite. After the game was over, we carefully put out the fire by covering it with decayed vegetation.

That night, Frank went to visit Uncle Louis. He noticed the forest fire while walking across the road from Uncle Louis's place. The next morning was Sunday and so I got up expecting to go to church. I had recently converted to Catholicism, and so I would be going to Los Gatos with Brother and Frank. I always looked forward to this. I came out of the bedroom and noticed the flames through the window in the Big Room. Just then Frank came in, all covered with soot and ashes. He had been fighting the fire most of the night. Frank was only fourteen, but he was so tall he looked grown up to me.

I pointed at the fire through the window and said, "Wh-wh-wh-wh-what's that?"

Uncle Louis must have told him about seeing us with the candles the day before, because Frank just smiled knowingly.

Clara had taken Mama to visit her childhood home in Oregon. Mama was in a great mood when she got back. Someone must have told her about the fire in the redwood grove, because she unexpectedly asked, "Margaret, you didn't have anything to do with that fire in the redwood grove, did you?"

"Who me?" I asked innocently, stalling for time.

Mama said, "Oh, I didn't think so, dear."

LISTENING IN ON THE
PARTY LINE

GOSSIP SPREAD QUICKLY through the mountain grape vine, not least of all due to our telephone system which was one of the old party lines. We had seven parties on our line, and one operator. "Central" was located at the Burrell General Store. Mrs. Sharp was the operator for years and years. (She was very petite and looked like an old fashioned doll with long ringlets.) When you wanted to make a call, you cranked a little handle on the side of your phone. One long ring was for the operator. However, if you just wanted to call someone on the same line, you could crank out the number yourself.[60] You couldn't call out if the line was occupied. Unless you had an emergency, all you could do was ask the long-winded talkers if they would hang up for a few minutes so you could make your call.

Theoretically, you were only supposed to pick up when you heard your own ring. However, you could pick up and listen in on the conversation whenever a call came in for anyone on your line. Naturally, the temptation was irresistible for most, and everyone recognized by the ring who was being called and what sort of juicy gossip they might hear.[61] Whenever you were on the line, you could hear the click,

---

[60] Our ring was two longs and two shorts. That's what we heard whether the call was coming from someone on our own line, or whether Mrs. Sharp had transferred a call to us from someone on the outside. (Au.)

[61] The 900 "party line" numbers of today, although technically quite different, seem to operate on the same principle that listening in on other people's conversations can be more interesting than engaging in your own conversation. Of course, today's "party lines" have additional costs built in. (Ed.)

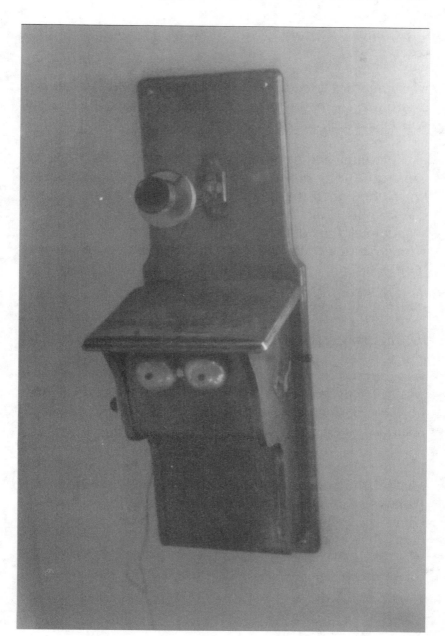

An old fashioned phone. If you wanted to call someone on your own line, you cranked out the number yourself with the handle on the right.

click, click as all of the different parties picked up their receivers.

Some people developed a verbal code. My sister Mary and her friend Jeanne Eggleston spoke Pig Latin to each other. There were two foreign ladies who spoke Slovakian with each other, and this was very irritating to those who tried to listen in.

Mama and Aunt Ida put booze into their minced pie. This was during prohibition, and they didn't want others to know about their illegal activities. Also, even if the country hadn't gone "dry," it would still have been considered scandalous if the other people on the line had heard the two women asking each other for whiskey or brandy. So instead they asked each other for a little coffee or tea to put in their minced pie. This got the whole mountains buzzing. Everyone wanted their recipe!

There were many petty jealousies and animosities in the mountains. These would be aired on the party line for everyone's benefit. Mrs. Godsman, the Reverend's wife, was referred to as the hypocrite. Mrs. King, our neighbor, was called the gossip. "I'll bet the Gossip is on the line," Aunt Ida would say to Mama. "I am not!" Mrs. King would respond.

Sometimes picking up the party line wasn't so funny, like the time Mama picked up the phone (she said she mistook the ring for our own) and found out that Aunt Carlie, Papa's sister, had died. One of Carlie's neighbors in Willow Glen was calling our neighbor, Doris Fidel, to ask her to break the news to us gently.

STORE BOUGHT TEETH, AND OTHER MAIL TALES

UNCLE WILL, the mail carrier, had many stories about his years on the rural route. He was the one who usually found the elderly in their beds, or wherever, when they had expired. If they didn't come to the mail box for their mail after three or four days, he would go into their homes. (No one in the mountains ever locked their homes back then.) Sometimes they weren't dead, but had only taken a turn for the worse. In that case, he would tell the next neighbor down the road to check in on them.

One of the funniest stories I've ever heard regarding Uncle Will's mail route was told to me by my cousin Phyllis. One of the men on his route had sent away for some store bought teeth from the east. First, they sent him a tube of some thick, gloppy stuff, which was used to make an impression of his real teeth. Then he went into town and had his teeth extracted by Painless Parker. Then, according to the instructions, he was to make another set of impressions of his gums. After he sent both of these impressions to the company in the east, all he had to do was sit back and wait for his new teeth. They only cost four dollars, which was a real bargain, even in those days.

After sending for his new teeth, he could hardly contain himself. He met Uncle Will at the mailbox every day, asking, "Have they come yet?" Finally, they came....The next day he met Uncle Will, he had a big club in his hands. He raised it and started beating on the car! Uncle Will traded in his car every year, as the mail route was hard on it, so his car was undoubtedly in good shape...before the man started to club it, that is. He dented the car all up before Will could start the engine and get away. The man didn't like his new teeth!

Uncle Will took one quick look back as he pulled away as fast as he could, before he got his windshield smashed in. He said the man looked like Dracula.

The moral of this story is: never come bearing bad news, or inferior merchandise.

THE RURAL MAIL ROUTE provided him with many such stories. Sometimes we had to wait a long time for them, as he would not spread gossip or say anything about someone who was still living in the area. He told about the time Salvadore got a special delivery letter, but since he had no permanent residence and could not be located, Will took the letter to the Los Gatos Post Office.

The next time he saw Salvadore, he told him about the letter. Salvadore walked all the way to Los Gatos, about fourteen miles down the Old San Jose Road. The postal clerk told him they had sent it to San Francisco.

The next day, Salvadore started walking to San Francisco. He arrived, hot, dirty and swearing. When he asked about his letter, they said they had sent it back to the sender. Salvadore really started to swear, and he threatened to blow up the post office with a stick of dynamite!

BROTHER CONSIDERED UNCLE WILL the best mail carrier the Santa Cruz Mountains ever had. His punctuality was such that you could set your watch by him, except on Sundays. But even Brother received an annoying letter from Will's hands once.

When Brother was twenty-two, fifteen-year-old Phyllis and nineteen-year-old Mary sent him a joke letter. He pretended not to know who sent it, but he made it known that as soon as he discovered who had done the dastardly deed, he was going to get a lawyer and sue them. Phyllis and Mary had a few anxious weeks until the fruit harvest and Brother's marriage overshadowed the whole affair.

Uncle Will, who took his job very seriously, admonished us all not to use the U.S. mails so frivolously.

Here is the letter:

January 10, 1938

Mr. Adolphus Rapp
Route 2 Box 225
Los Gatos, Calif.

Dear Mr. Rapp:

We find it our painful duty to inform you that a new streptococcus of the speciesyoglathopipia has been discovered and is on your property as a result of raising a low grade of swine—pigs to you. We have studied the pigs from the same source as yours and we find that the people who used the meat of the pigs and the bristles in brushes have become stricken with a most terrible desease with devastating results.

The period of incubation of the streptococcus is one to ten years. The first symptoms are falling hair and decaying teeth. This is followed by the skin turning a queer greenish tint which is luminous at night. Yellow crusts form on the eyes. Queer babblings come forth from the oral cavity. The face swells up, the nose flattening and giving the face a round, shiney, smoothe surface, except for the eyes which pop. The remaining fringe of hair becomes blue and the ears shrivel into small balls. The body goes into writhing, twitching convultions at the sight of one of the opposite sex. The bones crackle and the gums chatter while foam appears at the mouth. When the person is startled, water comes pouring out of his ears. His bones become elastic and he is able to fold up in numerous unheard of places. Toenails and fingernails drop out, while the fingers and toes grow together. When this condition is reached, death follows. Now you, dear sir, wouldn't want this to happen to you. Always keep fit—always keep trim by taking Dr. Pierce's Little Liver Pills. Use them consistently and you will never come down with Paraphenglenediamine.

Very truly yours,
LYDIA E. PINKMAN
AND CO.

Fussin' Feudin' and a Fightin' — Or More Mail Tales

IT ALL STARTED SO INNOCENTLY. Aunt Lydia, our swearing aunt, wrote a letter to Aunt May. Uncle Will Hurney, Mama's brother-in-law, was the mail carrier. He delivered the letter to Mama because it looked like the letter was addressed to Mrs. A. Rapp instead of May H. Rapp.

When Mama opened the letter the salutation was, "Hello Darling," so naturally she didn't realize it wasn't meant for her eyes. Mama thought it was such a nice letter. In fact, it was the nicest letter she had ever gotten from Lydia. So Mama sent it on to my sister Clara.

Meanwhile, Lydia wondered why May hadn't written her back. She wrote May and asked her why the hell she hadn't answered her letter. May wrote back that she hadn't received a letter from her in a long while. Lydia wrote May again saying that she had just gotten a letter from Emma thanking her for the dear, sweet letter. The only thing was, Lydia hadn't written to Emma. She had written to May. "How in the *&@% did Emma get that letter?"

May contacted Will Hurney and asked him if a letter had come from Lydia lately. Since Aunt May had been deaf for many years, all Uncle Will could do was nod his head. Aunt May was hopping mad!

She contacted Mama and found out the letter wasn't even in her possession anymore, as she had passed it onto Clara. Aunt May, in her anger, yelled at Mama and told her she had committed a federal offense, and might even go to prison for life for mail theft. Mama and Aunt May never spoke to each other again, although they just lived across the road from one other.

May quickly realized she was the loser in this feud, as Mama used to drive her into town. She broke down and asked Frank if he could patch things up between them. Frank told her there were some personalities that just didn't get along. He thought this was a prime example of just such a personality conflict.

PAPA'S KITCHEN

WHETHER IT WAS WARTIME OR DEPRESSION TIME, Papa always managed to keep his large family well fed. One of Clara's earliest memories was discovering that Papa was hoarding food staples such as flour and sugar during World War I, although, at three years old, she was too young to understand the implications of what she saw.

"I remember Papa going up into the attic and coming down with a sack of white flour," Clara said. "When Mama saw me watching, she was aghast and admonished me not to tell anyone. It was her job to see that none of us were around when Papa got the flour.

"Mr. Napier from the Laurel store had told Papa, because of the war, there was going to be a shortage of white flour and, as he had a large family, he should lay in a supply. Most people had to use brown flour. I'm sure Mrs. Husbands,[62] who took care of us when Mama was sick or having babies, always used brown flour."

Papa probably didn't consider this hoarding unpatriotic, but merely a precautionary measure to make sure everyone in his large household ate all right.

A FEW WEEKS AFTER Grandma and Grandpa's fiftieth wedding anniversary, in 1926, Mama confided to her brother-in-law Ernest that Papa hadn't been feeling too well, but that he refused to go to a doctor. Ernest lured Papa into his medical office by telling him he wanted to show Papa all of his new fangled equipment. He tried some of it out on Papa and

---

[62] This was very likely Mary Elizabeth Husbands, who was born in England in 1831 and lived in California the last twenty-five years of her life, according to county records. (Ed.)

discovered that his blood pressure was sky high. Papa had worked incredibly hard all of his life, and he had a lot of worries. Besides all of his family responsibilities—first to his little sisters and his ailing mother, and then to his own large family—Papa had followed a heavy plow all over his property for many years, the equivalent of twenty-five miles a day. Papa had always done the plowing himself.

At the time Ernest checked him out, Papa was fifty-four. Ernest told him if he didn't slow down and learn to relax he only had about three years to live, at the most. Papa heeded his advice. He basically handed the running of the farm over to Mama. The older girls, Elizabeth and Emma Mae, took over most of the cooking for the family and the hired hands. Papa took care of the smaller children and puttered around the house.

He lived until he was ninety-four, outliving Ernest and four other doctors. (When he told this to the sixth doctor, who was only in his mid-fifties, the doctor said, "Well what did you come to me for?")

Papa basically retired in 1926. In 1932, like almost everybody else, he was short of money. He took out a large loan from the First National Bank in Los Gatos at seven percent interest. This was a high interest rate for that time, but he needed the money to continue running the farm and to look after the family until he could get money for his crops. He used his PG&E stock for collateral.

The following year, in February, 1933, the bank sent a letter saying: "Some time ago you gave us a selling order for a portion of your P.G.&E. Co. shares, but the trend of the market would indicate that it will be some time before your figure is reached. In view of the fact that we have carried your note for some time now and the value of the collateral is only slightly more than the principal of the note, we believe you should make some plan to reduce the principal between now and the next due date on March 31."

To complicate matters, the bank addressed and sent this letter to Papa's brother Otto. Otto's wife Lydia guessed that the letter might be concerning her brother-in-law, as she heard him mention that he had some PG&E stock and knew he did business at the First National Bank. She sent the letter on to Papa, along with a personal note about her latest success with breeding chickens.

When the letter from the bank finally reached my parents, Mama feared that Papa would have a heart attack from the strain of worrying over how to pay off this loan. She went and spoke to Mr. Hamsher at the First National Bank, and told him her husband was worrying himself to death over his loan. Mr. Hamsher told her to go home and tell Adolph not to worry.

ALTHOUGH PAPA was technically retired for as long as I can remember, he kept active. I'm sure that contributed to his long life. He planted and pruned trees, slaughtered the pigs, and cooked many of the family meals. Breakfast was his specialty.

Slaughtering the pigs was a big job; and afterwards every part of the pig was used. He, Brother, and usually one other helper, were involved. First they put a big cauldron of water to boil on an open fire. Then the pig was shot in the head. (That's when I ran and hid, because I could hear the pig squealing.) If the pig seemed to be suffering, they would wop it over the head with the side of an axe, or a sledge hammer.

Once the pig was sufficiently dead, they would slit it down the stomach and take out its entrails. Then they put it in a cauldron of boiling water for a couple of minutes. After they took it out, they scraped off all of the hair. They cleaned the entrails and used them as casing for the sausages. (I had to help with this, and I thought it was disgusting.)

The liver was cooked and ground into liverwurst, and stuffed into the casings. Papa cured the hams. In the original recipe, he would smoke them for days in our smoke house, but later he used special salts for curing ham.

The two hams were from the pig's rump. The shoulders were usually had as a roast. The bacon came from the pig's side, under the ribs, and Papa had a special way of preparing this, too.

Papa would cut off the pigs head and boil it for head cheese. First he would boil it until all of the meat fell off the

Soooey! It's hog killing time. From l. to r.: Louis, Otto and Adolph Rapp, c. 1915.

bones, then he added spices and put it into a loaf pan. It became gelatinous and could be sliced. Papa found this to be a rare delicacy. I thought otherwise.

The pig's feet were cleaned, boiled and pickled. This was another delicacy I could do without.

Papa saved the pig's brains for his personal favorite treat—scrambling them with eggs. He was the only one who ate this one. The pig's brains could only be preserved for two or three days, so Papa generally scooped these right out and scrambled them up immediately.

Papa always had several days work cut out for him after the pig was slaughtered. We didn't have a refrigerator until I was twelve years old, so all of the meat had to be cured by either salting or smoking it.

PAPA ALSO MADE THE BEST SAUERKRAUT. He would take about twenty heads of cabbage and slice them up on a slicer. Then he put it all into a deep crock and added lots of salt. He covered it with a board and put a brick on top to weigh it down. This kept the air out and prevented the cabbage from getting mouldy. He left it for a long time, testing it every few days when he thought it was almost ready. Once he felt it was ready, he could dip in and get as much as he needed for dinner. He would rinse off the salt and boil it. It was especially good cooked with pork!

At the end of summer, he would cure the surplus eggs and store them in water glass, a powder which dissolved in water and made a clear, syrupy liquid. This kept the air from getting through the eggshells.

Papa grew his own horseradish roots. I helped him grind them, and the whole house would reek of horseradish. It made tears stream down our faces, a hundred times more so than onions generally do. After it was ground, he added a little vinegar and sealed it in jars. This horseradish always took your breath away. It was much stronger than what you buy in a grocery store today. It was particularly good with beef; and it always seemed to be a good cold cure.

Papa had a huge corn field in the back of the property. He raised several different kinds of corn: some for the chickens, some for the pigs, and some for us. He even raised popcorn. (The only kind of corn that pops.)

He had a huge vegetable garden on the site where the old barn burned down. He never had to add manure, and the vegetables grew to prize-winning proportions. They tasted so sweet. I've never tasted string beans like those since. He also had unusual things in his garden, such as goose berries. They made fantastic pies. He also raised blackberries and raspberries.

Mama did most of the canning and pie making, but Papa loved to make apple butter. He cooked the apples until they were the consistency of soft butter. Then he added cinnamon and cloves and a dash of nutmeg.

AFTER THE BOYS HAD MILKED THE COWS, the milk was put into pans that went into the cooler. For several days afterwards, the cream was skimmed off of the top and put into the butter churn. Three or four days later, we had enough cream to start churning the butter. After the butter was removed from the churn, it was rinsed. Then it was placed into a bowl and stirred with a wooden spoon until it formed a solid mass.

Little specks of butter were left in the whey at the bottom of the churn. This was how the original buttermilk was derived. The modern version is cultured and thicker, and has a different flavor.

Papa also liked clabbered milk, which had turned sour and become thick, like yogurt.

When Papa got a sweet tooth, he would make butter-milk donuts, which he fried in deep fat. He loved to bake apple fritters.

When I was nine, I had my appendix out. Before that I usually got stomach aches, and so I couldn't eat a lot of Papa's rich food. I did, however, love to drink buttermilk with him.

PAPA ALSO MADE WINE, beer and rootbeer. Children always loved to help out in the rootbeer making process. Their job was to wash and sterilize the bottles. Papa mixed the rootbeer with an extract and water, in the correct proportions. Like

A slice of farm life — Papa brings in the cow, c. 1915.

beer, rootbeer ferments inside the bottles. (Although the process for making beer is otherwise much more complex than that of making rootbeer.)

Papa made these things throughout his life. First his children were helpers, then his grandchildren assisted with the bottle washing. My son Steve reminded me of one time when he and his brothers helped Papa make rootbeer. Papa called a few days later and said, "You all never mind coming up for that rootbeer. All the bottles exploded."

Papa loved his chickens. You could always see him in the chicken coop early in the morning and at dusk. Once, my son Ken hatched a chicken in his Chick-U-Bator. When it got too big for our suburban home, he took it to the ranch. Papa always reported back to Ken, saying, "Yes siree Ken, that hen of yours lays every day of the week, and twice on Sundays."

PAPA'S LAST MAJOR PROJECT was to clear all of the brush and poison oak out of the madrone grove and build a little park for his many grandchildren. Papa bought a children's swing set, hung a hammock, and put up picnic tables. It was quickly dubbed "Grandpa's Park."

Sometimes when you get older, it is easier to remember childhood memories. Papa told me once about going rabbit hunting in Missouri with an uncle of his. He said he had dreamed about this hunting trip the night before. He was only three at the time he went, and he was ninety-three when he had this dream. I was amazed his mind had stored that memory for ninety years.

I remember when I was a child, listening to him sing German lullabies to put me to sleep. Although German had been his first language and he spoke it as long as his mother was alive, he had forgotten most of it over the years. But he still remembered the lullabies he had heard when he was young.

SOME CURTAINS FALL

DEATH ALWAYS COMES IN THREES.
One April Fools' Day, when I was twelve, I called Uncle Louis up and told him there was a package in his mail box. Uncle Louis was a good sport and lots of fun to tease. This day he told me he didn't feel very well and asked me if I would bring the package down to his house. I yelled, "April Fools!" and hung up. He died seven days later.

When Aunt Carlie heard her brother had died, she fainted. She had a heart attack and died herself, a couple of days later.

Aunt Carlie's funeral was first, as we were waiting for one of Aunt May's relatives to come from the east for Louis's funeral. We stayed with relatives overnight between the two funerals.

When we got home after the second funeral, I found out my favorite dog had eaten some rat poison and died. Papa and I had a funeral for him. We buried him in Papa's garden, and Papa covered his grave with an upside down wash tub to mark the site.

I don't know if this was the final straw or what, but I felt more upset over the loss of my dog than I did over the loss of my aunt and uncle. He used to keep my feet warm by sleeping under the covers at night.

Later that same year, the day after Thanksgiving, Brother came to our house to tell us that Uncle Otto had died the night before. Mama and I were sitting on the East Porch, and Papa was feeding his chickens. Mama told Brother to go tell his father about Otto.

Papa was smiling as Brother approached him. We couldn't hear what Brother said, but I'll never forget the look of raw grief that came over Papa's face. In seven months, he

Louis Rapp, in his later years.

had lost three of his brothers and sisters.

Papa and his last remaining sister, Rena, both lived many years after that. Aunt Rena lived until she was seventy-nine. Papa was almost ninety-five when he died.

Otto and Lydia Rapp, c. 1910s.

LIFE IN THE '30s

MAMA TRIED TO SHIELD me from sensational news headlines. Unfortunately (or fortunately) I could read at a very early age and had excellent hearing, so not much escaped me. One of the sensational things that happened in the thirties that had a life-long effect on me was the Lindbergh kidnapping. Charles Lindbergh was famous for his solo flight across the Atlantic in 1927. When his infant son was kidnapped from his crib in March of 1932, it was daily news until April of 1936, when Bruno Hauptman, who had been convicted of this crime, was executed. This crime made kidnapping a federal offense.

Mama also tried to shelter me from the shocking news of the lynching right near us, in San Jose. The men accused of kidnapping and murdering the son of the owners of Hart's department store was removed from the jail and taken across the street to Saint James Park and lynched on the spot. This was in 1933. Saint James Park has never been the same since. I sometimes heard Mama and Delphine Parker whispering about this.

Clara tells of this incident: "When the Hart's son was murdered, it was a great sensational tragedy. The kidnappers were caught and jailed. The emotional feeling was so strong that they had to move them to another jail. However, before the change took place, some enraged citizens took them and hung them on a palm tree in Saint James Park.

"Emma Mae was nursing at O'Connor's hospital a few miles away, and could hear the angry roar of the mob! The folks and I were visiting Jack and Elizabeth, and Jack had them get down on their knees to pray for their souls as well as the guilty ones causing and doing the hanging."

The bad feelings from that lynching have carried over

through the years without people really understanding why the park seemed dreary, ugly, and yes—sinister!

I was at St. James Park one evening in the sixties when Bobbie Kennedy was running for president. He was supposed to arrive at six in the evening to make a speech. He was an hour or so late in arriving. The people were starting to grumble and make angry sounds which began to swell. Bobbie Kennedy arrived and flashed his smile, which instantly soothed the feelings of the crowd. He said, "There hasn't been a lynching here since 1933. Please, let's not repeat that dreadful incident!"

Then there were the headlines about the disappearance in July, 1937 of Amelia Earhart, who had soloed over the Pacific in 1935. She was attempting an around the world flight when she went down, and she was never heard from again.

I was nine years old and visiting my cousin Janet in Stockton the summer Will Rogers died in an air plane crash. That was August, 1935. I saw the glaring headlines on that summer's day, and I remember how sad it made me feel. I had liked his movies. He had a lot of homespun wisdom.

WHEN I WAS A CHILD, Mama did not seem to have the word "sex" in her vocabulary. That was where our education fell short. We had no sex education, except what we saw on the farm, read about in magazines, or saw in the movies. The movies were not very enlightening. In the thirties, there were only fade outs to make us think that something—some mysterious, wonderful something—happened.

I remember one late summer's day, after the cousins and farm hands had left for the summer and before school started. It was a sad, hot, boring day. Frank was probably bored too, or perhaps he only wanted to use the facilities. I was sitting on the throne, probably hoping to avoid doing the dishes, when Frank picked up a bucket of water and threw it in through the screen that went across the top edge of one side of the outhouse.

I gasped, running out the door screaming and madder than a wet hen. In fact, at that moment, I knew exactly what one felt like. I remember deliberately taking my wet wailing little body into the house where I knew Mama could be found. I would just happen to cross her path and of course she would ask me, "What happened to you?" I would have to tell her. It wouldn't be the same as voluntarily tattling on Frank, now would it? As I carried out this hastily devised plan, a little voice in the back of my head said, "you'll be sorry!"

Let's go back now, to a school day some two years prior to this event. I was six years old and it was my first year of walking up the long two miles to Highland Grammar School. I was walking along with a male class mate who was seven years old at the time. We decided to take off all our clothes and continue our walk. Just then my brother Frank decided to come back around the bend and see what was taking me so long. Frank had been admonished to look out for his little sister. When he saw me and this little boy walking along in the buff, he said, "If you ever tell Mama anything on me, I will tell her about this."

I had tucked this piece of blackmail away, but it had started to fade somewhat until this most eventful day in August, 1934. The instant that Mama asked, and I told, I knew I'd better make tracks.

It was only a moment or so after she had called Frank in, that I heard her calling my name. I knew I might as well come out and face the music. Since it was summertime, and our beds were still out on the Big Porch, Mama stalled for time. She said, "You go get in bed and don't come out for supper." Mama rarely punished us, so this felt very severe. "And you stay there until I call you!" she added.

In the meantime, Papa and Brother had gone to town to buy a new tractor, and they could be heard driving the truck with the tractor in it up the long driveway. Mama said, "Get up now and behave yourself. Not a word of this to Papa." Mama was not up to explaining my dreadful crime to him. Frank's crime had turned into a minor misdemeanor, and remained unpunished.

Just as all this was going on, Frank was taking the old plough horse down to the well in the redwood grove to drink some water. The horse looked up and saw the truck with the

Margaret and Frank Rapp, 1929.

tractor going by, and I suppose he knew his useful days were over. He laid right down and died.

The moral of this story is: If there are enough diversionary tactics, seemingly major problems become unimportant. With the arrival of the new tractor, and the death of the old plow horse, my heinous crime was transformed into a misdemeanor, and promptly forgotten.

Years later, when I was nineteen and laughingly discussing this episode with Frank, he said, "Yeah Maggie, I shouldn't have told on you." This might have been why he never mentioned the incident of the fire that he (rightly) assumed I had caused in the redwoods when I was ten years old.

MAMA WAS VERY PATIENT in teaching us how to cook. Once she let me follow a recipe for vanilla pudding. The first time I made it, it was much too salty. Mama just told me to try again dear, "and use a little less salt." I made it again, this time cutting the salt in half. She tasted it again and said, "It's still too salty dear." Then she let me try again because, "I had to learn sometime." The third time I didn't put any salt in—or so I thought. When Mama tasted it this time she spat it out and said, "Give it up, Margaret!" We discovered that the pan of white stuff on the table, which I thought was sugar, was actually salt. I didn't have any vanilla pudding that day.

Another peculiar incident occurred in our kitchen involving salt. Mama asked Mary to put a level teaspoon of salt in the beans that were cooking on the stove. Mary put *eleven* teaspoons of salt in the beans. We didn't have any beans that day.

The neighbor children and cousins loved to come to our house, as Mama would let us experiment in the kitchen. I remember the time we made taffy. It got so hard on the plate, where it was cooling, that we couldn't get it off and we had to throw the plate away.

One of the most exciting cooking experiences occurred when Mama was trying out her new pressure cooker. (I've been afraid of them ever since.) She was cooking applesauce. I think the directions warned against cooking applesauce, but you only read the directions when you couldn't figure it out by yourself. The safety valve got all plugged up with the thick applesauce, and the lid blew clear off! It went straight through the square vent in the ceiling, where the chimney for the wood stove used to be. The lid went straight up and landed on top of the roof. You might say this was one time when Mama literally "blew her lid."

Our gasoline iron should have been in a museum. I don't know what kept it from exploding. It worked on the same principal as the gasoline lantern. Air had to be pumped in and the little gasoline tank on the back of the iron filled with fuel. After you lit it, you regulated it for a blue flame. Then you regulated it for heat. I remember it being very temperamental and I was always a little afraid of that, too.

Elizabeth told me of a thermal cooker they had, although I don't remember it. Elizabeth said it looked like a fine piece of furniture, such as a cedar chest. Inside were layers of insulation. A few red hot bricks, which had been heated on the wood stove, were placed inside on a metal liner around a pan of food and the lid bolted down tightly. After several hours, you opened the lid and—*voila!*—a delicious meal was ready.

WE ALWAYS HAD OUR WEEKLY BATHS on Saturday nights, whether we were dirty or not. The tub was brought into the kitchen by the warm stove, and the water was heated on the wood burning stove. Sometimes two of us used the same wash water, and then rinsed off with clear water. Water was always scarce. We had two bathtubs built into the house, but they were only used on summer days when it was warm, as it was too far to carry heated water from the kitchen.

We had a wash house, separate from the main house, where our Rube Goldberg-like washer was stored. The washer worked with electricity, whenever we had electricity. The wringer was turned on by hand, for safety reasons, and stuck out from the side of the washer. Mama seldom did the wash there when I was growing up. The family was smaller by then, and she preferred the old washboard. The ridges on the wash board were good for rubbing extra soiled overalls

Stanley Fidel "holds up" his sister Marna Lou (far r.) and Margaret.

or socks on, instead of using your knuckles.

Some of the everyday problems, which seemed minor to me, but certainly were major from Mama's and Papa's standpoint, included keeping the water tank filled with water.[63] Sometimes when the well went dry, we had to haul water. Also, the long, winding driveway up to our house had to be periodically oiled and graveled. Wood for the fire had to be chopped and carried into the house.

Some of the vendors who braved the narrow mountain roads included the fish man, who came with his open, fishy smelling truck. On a hot day, you could smell it a mile away. There was also Mr. Rhoades, the butcher, who was very generous about handing out raw weiners to the children he met along the way. (I'm sure health officials would shudder at this thought today!) The grocer Mr. Rushton drove up from Soquel once a week, during the '30s and '40s. "The Watkins man," who worked for the Watkins company, made regular rounds too. I remember the wonderful odors of the lemon and vanilla extract he always had us smell.

Then there was another kind of merchant who braved the back roads. I still remember the smell of the hearse when the undertaker, Mr. Place, would stop and give me a ride home. When I was growing up in the Santa Cruz Mountains, we were not admonished to decline rides from strangers, as actually, there were no strangers.

AT NIGHT, we all sat around our Philco radio and listened to the radio shows. There were so many. There was: "Fibber McGee and Molly," "Amos and Andy," "Lum and Abner, and Their Jot 'Em Down Store." There were radio personalities like Fred Allen, Jack Benny, George Burns and Gracie Allen. Then there was "Jack Armstrong, The All American Boy," "Li'l Orphan Annie," "I Love a Mystery," and "Death Valley Days." I could go on and on, but these were some of our favorites.

---

[63] This is always a problem in the Santa Cruz Mountains, where water is scarce, especially in sumers up until the rainy season begins. (Ed.)

Once, when we were listening to "Henry Aldrich" (he was always getting into scrapes), Mama glanced at me and my cousin Janet and said to Papa, "These are our 'Henry Aldriches.'" Janet and I had just gotten into trouble for buying penny candy, cutting it in half, and then re-wrapping it and selling it for a penny. Mama and Papa didn't think we should do that.

Frank still loves to hear two stories involving Mama and me. One was when I was nine years old, and just coming down with the measles. Mama had me set up in the pantry during the day while she was working in the kitchen. I had been lying there quietly, listening to a bubble in my stomach. I thought I was listening to my heart beating. Suddenly it stopped. I leaped across the floor landing in the kitchen. Mama grabbed a bed pan and said, "If you want to throw—" I cut her off by screaming, "No, my heart stopped beating!" Mama thought that was impossible, or else I wouldn't be hopping around. But then she must have thought of the way chickens still run around after their heads are chopped off. Anyway, I did alarm her. She ran out to the orchard, where Papa was, and said, "Margaret said her heart stopped beating!"

The other story Frank loves is the one about the little girl who chased her mother around the pool table. You see, I was dreadfully afraid of loud noises when I was little. One time during an electrical storm, I got up and started running around the pool table in the Big Room. Mama got up and started running around to try to catch me. Since I could run faster than Mama, Frank said it looked like I was chasing her.

Frank always said this was the funniest thing he ever saw in his life, with the only possible exception being the time the goat chased me into Elizabeth's cottage when I was four years old.[64] The goat had no intention of hurting me. He just put his head down as if he was going to butt me, and I took off running and screaming. Every time he almost caught up with me, the goat stopped and let me get a little farther

---

[64] This was the same goat Frank had been so afraid of four years earlier, when Brother made him "take it in." (Au.)

Adolph Rapp Jr., "Brother," in a Santa Cruz County Farm Bureau photo, c. 1930s.

ahead. Elizabeth, hearing me scream, opened her cottage door and I ran in. I had swallowed my gum and my shoes had fallen off.

I threw those stories in just for you, Frank.

So you see, although growing up on a farm during the depression had its traumas, it certainly had its fun times, too.

DISCORD IN THE HARMONY MISSIONARY SOCIETY

IN HER MIDDLE YEARS, Mama had more time to become politically active in the Skyland community. She belonged to the Home Department (the women's branch of the Farm Bureau), the School Board, and the Harmony Missionary Society, of which she was both president and vice-president at various times.

Once a woman came up from the city of Santa Cruz to advise the ladies of the Home Department on the evils of davenports, an early word for sofa. This was in the 1920s, and none of the farm women had one yet—but there was always a chance that one of them might get the idea to order a davenport through the Sears and Roebuck Catalogue. The woman from Santa Cruz said davenports were a health hazard, collecting dust and creating a fertile breeding ground for bacteria. In addition, they encouraged laziness and sloth. Mama went right home and ordered a davenport. Some of my fondest memories are of Mama curled up on the davenport, rubbing her curly brown hair and telling one of her long stories. If the story became too exciting, she would hop up and begin acting it out for us.

One time in 1934, Mama had a man come to our house to demonstrate Wearever Aluminum Cookware. The sales pitch for Wearever was that you only needed a teaspoon of water on low heat and the vegetables would steam in their own juices. Mama invited all of the neighbors. The gimmick was that the salesman provided the food and everyone present got a free meal. After the cooking demonstration, came the big sales pitch. Mama was so excited that she brought the whole pan full of potatoes into the parlor to show the guests.

"See!" she said, "These were cooked entirely without water!" She tipped the pan just a little too far, and all of the potatoes fell onto the dusty davenport. Mama never missed a beat. She scooped them back into the pan and said, "Never mind. There are plenty more out in the kitchen."

During all of this excitement, Emma Mae telephoned Mama to tell her she had passed her state board and would receive a license as a registered nurse. Mama was so overwhelmed by all of this she just said, "That's nice, dear." Emma Mae was hurt because Mama wasn't more enthusiastic about her achievement.

WITHOUT A DOUBT, Mama's biggest involvement in the Skyland community was her work with the Harmony Missionary Society. As far as I could see, they mainly got together and pieced quilts for the Ming Quong Home in Los Gatos.[65] The ladies of the Harmony Missionary Society provided the home with quilts, and themselves with an excuse to get together and gossip, say a few prayers, and have some delicious desserts. Every time Mama came home from one of her meetings, she would act out what all of the ladies had said, imitating each of their voices and mannerisms perfectly.

Once a month, the ladies all prepared the most delicious cakes in their wood burning stoves, to impress the other ladies of the society. The dessert I remember best was Adele Grandeman's angel food cake. At each meeting, one of the ladies would be chosen to lead the others in prayer before they partook of their refreshments. This always came at the end of a long, tiring session of quilting.

Then the Harmony Missionary Society hit a flat note! There was a squabble among some of the members. Mrs. Godsman split off and formed a new circle, or, as she claimed, continued the work of the Harmony Missionary Society. Mama, and some of the other members, also continued the work of the Harmony Missionary Society. Both

[65] At that time, this was a home for Chinese orphans. Today, it is a home for retarded children. (Au.)

The ladies of the Harmony Missionary Society. Back row l. to r.: May Rapp, Maude Clough, Mrs. van Harlenger, Emma Rapp (Mama), Winifred Wragg. Front row l. to r.: Adele Grandeman, Josie Clough and a young Margaret Rapp, 1937.

groups claimed to be the *true* Harmony Missionary Society. Among some of the ladies remaining in Mama's group were Kitty Mason, Annie Steffans, Winnifred Wragg, Adele Grandeman, Caroline Waltz, and of course Mama's dearest friend, Delphine Parker, who was president of the new, *true* Harmony Missionary Society.

Both of the groups of ladies continued their quilting bees. But of course the two societies with the same name never interacted.

The meeting I shall never forget was held at our house. Mama was leading the ladies in a solemn prayer. I was wishing it would end so we could get on with the cake! Salvadore burst in through the door and hollered, "Godammit! Isn't anyone home?" He had probably been knocking for some time, but couldn't be heard over the noise of the ladies' gabbing. Mama was mortified. Mrs. Parker teased her for a long time after that episode, insisting that Mama had staged his entrance.

SCHOOL DAYS

MAMA WAS A SCHOOL BOARD TRUSTEE for nine years, three of those as clerk. The board determined everything from whom to hire, to what their duties and their pay would be, to when school holidays would be, to budget expenditures.

When Mrs. Eggleston was hired, the board enacted a rule that after a teacher taught a certain amount of time, she couldn't be fired. Mrs. Eggleston said she probably wouldn't teach more than five or six years anyway, as her husband was bedridden with tuberculosis. She taught at Highland School for sixteen years, receiving one hundred dollars a month for teaching and another twenty dollars for janitorial work.

In order to keep the school open, there had to be at least six pupils. One year, enrollment fell short by one pupil. Frank was only five years old at the time, and was admitted to the first grade so the school would not be closed down. Frank began to cry when he thought Mrs. Eggleston wouldn't admit him, so naturally she accepted him.

Graduations were always a gala event, even though there was usually only one or two students in any given graduating class. Each eighth grader who was making the big step got to choose his or her own class colors and motto. The whole grammar school was involved in the recital. Clara remembered her grammar school graduation, and the unusual performance that accompanied it.

"At my graduation," she said, "along with other skits and monologues, was the main skit which Mrs. Eggleston wrote. She called it 'Vegetable Garden in Health Land.' I was the queen and had to decide between the beet, lettuce, carrot, potato, tomato, and squash, which was the most healthful, with each of the vegetables claiming that they were. We were all dressed up in crepe paper costumes resembling the respective vegetable. Of course the queen decided that each of them were needed for good health.

"Margaret, who was only three years old, was dressed in a butterfly costume, as was our cousin Barbara, who was five. Margaret was supposed to flit in and out among the vegetables, and then run off the stage. Margaret was a ham even then....She didn't want to stop flitting. So it took Mr. Eggleston at one wing and Mrs. Adams at another to pull her off the stage. Barbara had done what she was supposed to do."

Clara had another interesting impression to give of Brother's grammar school graduation:

"Brother was only thirteen when he graduated, but he was tall for his age. When Miss Young, the County Superintendent of Schools, gave out his diploma, she said that boys in the country were men when they graduated from grammar school. Mama must have thought that was a slur, as she had fire in her eyes when she cornered Miss Young, stating very emphatically, 'You know Miss Young, my boy is only thirteen.' Of course Miss Young apologized."

Until the last few months before my graduation, when a new boy in the mountains joined our school, Marjorie Wicht (pronounced "Wish") and I were the only two pupils in our grade level. We got to choose our class colors: Marjorie chose pink and I chose green. We chose sweet peas as our class flower since they are pink and green, and because Uncle Louis's place was profuse with sweet peas. In our recital, I played the witch in "Hansel and Gretle." Mama was not too pleased, as she wanted me to have a more glamorous role. I loved it though, because I could really sink my teeth into it. I scared all of the children in the audience. I also played the violin. Afterwards, a woman in the audience told me that my recital of "Brahm's Lullaby" had put her baby to sleep.

Sunday school was also an important part of education for the mountain kids. Clara remembered one year when the Sunday school teacher Mr. Brown decided to give the children of Highland, Burrell, Hester Creek, Summit and

Margaret stops flitting in her butterfly costume just long enough for this photo to be snapped.

Laurel schools a treat. There weren't many pupils in each school, twelve at most.

"Mr. Brown had the Pickwick Stage pick the children up at Skyland Church and Burrell School and take them to San Jose. He asked Mama and Mrs. Eggleston to be the chaperones. What a memorable trip it was! We were given a large key to the city of San Jose by Mayor Goodman. Then we visited the Judiciary Department and the jail. Then we sang hymns on Radio KQW. Then on to the Coffee Club to eat, which was always a treat. Our next stop was Hart's department store, where Mr. Hart gave us all ice cream cones."

Most mountain kids didn't get to town that often, maybe a couple of times a year. So events like this stuck out in their minds.

IN OUR FAMILY, we always made an annual trip to Santa Cruz, either to camp in a campground or to stay in a cabin at the beach. We would go to any lengths to get to Santa Cruz. Once the hired man, Mr. Cribs, canned the blackberries so we could go. They had ripened over night and Mama thought she was going to have to stay home and take care of them. But Mr. Cribbs said, "No, you all go along. I'll take care of them for you." Another time a tree had fallen across the road. The boys got out the axe and cut it in half so we could move it out of the way and get on the road.

The older children usually rode on the car's running boards. This wasn't dangerous, as Mama only drove about five miles an hour.

Mama gave us each fifty cents spending money when we got to the Santa Cruz Boardwalk. An ice cream cone only cost a nickel then. A ride cost ten cents. The smaller children weren't supposed to ride on the roller coaster. Once my cousin Phyllis rode on it without Mama's permission. When Mama told her she might have been killed, Phyllis said, "Oh, that's okay. My father would just sue them."

AFTER FINISHING GRAMMAR SCHOOL, if they wanted to attend high school, students from the Santa Cruz Mountains had to go to town. There was no school bus then.[66]

Mama and Papa thought they had taken care of this problem years before any of their children reached high school age. They bought ten acres in Morgan Hill to raise prunes on, with the intention of moving there to be closer to a high school when the time came. We went to Morgan Hill about once a year, because the trees needed to be pruned back in the fall. Mama and Papa built a garage on their Morgan Hill property, with the intention of building a house later on. However, Papa couldn't stand the idea of moving away from the Santa Cruz Mountains. When it came time for the teenagers to start high school, the garage stood alone on the ten acres in Morgan Hill. We did use it to camp in on our annual trek in the fall. I was about ten when I last remember going.

The teenagers in our family all lived in town so they could attend high school. They came home on weekends to help out on the farm.

When he was fifteen, Brother took over running the farm from Mama. This lightened her workload considerably. Although Mama had done much of the farm work for fifteen years, everyone took part. Being the youngest, I didn't feel the pressure until World War II, when hired men became so scarce that children were pressed into service on the farms. I didn't mind harvesting fruit. I enjoyed the feeling of productivity. It made me feel grown up. I remember many times during the harvest season, when the whole family would be awakened in the middle of the night because of rain. We had to move quickly to restack the prune trays, seeing our way through the dark by the headlights of the car. If we weren't fast enough, the drying fruit would be soaked and ruined.

Of course we also came home during school holidays. There were only two times when Papa wasn't with us on a

---

[66] In fact even today, high school students in the Santa Cruz Mountains commute to Los Gatos High School. There is a school bus now, and, of course, the old dirt roads have been paved. (Ed.)

The Kids Go to Town—Pickwick Stages took the mountain kids into Los Gatos. Mama, far left, acted as a chaperone. Jeanne Eggleston, the school teacher's daughter, is far left among the group of boys. Clara is just to the right of the town dignitary. Brother stands to her right, wearing a tie. Bob Hurney has his arm on Brother's shoulder.

holiday occasion. The first was in 1924, when he went to visit his old friends in Missouri and was gone longer than originally planned. Mama wrote him that he should stay as long as he was enjoying his visit. "Brother gets up every morning and makes the fires. He thinks he should," Mama wrote. "He says he is going to kill an old hen for our Thanksgiving dinner. It's nice to have a son."

Brother was only eight when he tried to kill a hen for Thanksgiving. Unfortunately, when he tried to chop off its head, he missed and just cut off the hen's beak. The old hen was terrified and flew up to the rafters. Uncle Louis had to come over and get the hen down and finish the job himself.

The second occasion was more tragic. Mama, Papa and Brother were all involved in a serious car accident in 1936. The shattered glass cut Papa's face from his temple down to his mouth, causing him to loose the sight in his right eye. He was in the hospital for a long time due to the loss of so much blood.

Uncle Louis came to our Christmas table that year and carved the turkey.

Mrs. Parker wrote to Mama on December 22, 1936 expressing her extreme condolences: "Dear Dear Friend, I've just been sick over your awful accident. I did so want to see you but could not find out where you were staying. I do pray Mr. Rapp isn't hurt as bad as the Dr. thinks he might be. Were you hurt? I phoned most every day to Clara Bell or the hospital but no one seemed to know just how badly Mr. Rapp was hurt. Write as soon as you find time and let me know how you both are.

"We missed you so much at the Missionary meeting. I think it's the first time you've been absent. We want to be very thankful it wasn't worse. And to happen just before Christmas!"

BEFORE LOS GATOS HIGH SCHOOL OPENED, students from the mountains attended Campbell High School. While Elizabeth went to Campbell High School, she lived in Willow Glen and worked for a family named Penniman, who lived on Carolyn

Street.[67] Emma Mae also attended Campbell High School, and she lived with and worked for a Campbell family named Field. Clara attended Campbell High her first two years, and also worked for the Fields.

Clara transferred to Los Gatos High School when it opened her junior year. The actress Olivia de Haviland was a classmate of hers. Clara sat behind Livvy, as she was called then, in Latin. Livvy's sister, the actress Joan Fontaine, also attended Los Gatos High.

During the years that Clara, Brother, Mary and Frank went to high school in Los Gatos, Mama rented an apartment for them for fifteen dollars a month. She would drive them to Los Gatos Sunday nights, and pick them up Friday nights. There was no school bus service for the students from the mountains. The school encouraged the mountain kids to attend, though. Out of the money that it received from the state for each pupil enrolled, the school passed along five dollars a month for each student who came down from the mountains to go to high school. The money was supposed to cover the cost of the gasoline to commute. However, the ranch was so far from town, Mama and Papa thought it made better sense to apply that money toward rent. At least during those years when they had three of their children attending high school at any one time, and sharing rent for fifteen dollars a month.

It sounds like every teenager's dream, to have their own apartment away from their parent's home. But there were hardships. Papa only gave each of them two dollars and fifty cents a week for living expenses. They had to supplement that with odd jobs after school. Mary only received twenty-five cents for an evening of babysitting. I didn't realize until much later how I cut into their tight budget sometimes. I took their milk bottles and turned them in for money to buy candy. Years later they told me they usually used the money from returns to buy food.

Mama felt secure that her kids were not completely

---

[67] Quite by coincidence, this same house is now owned by my cousin John Hurney, and his wife Eileen. (Au.)

without supervision. The apartment was upstairs in Mrs. Hewitt's home. She had been a childhood friend of Mama's.

Frank was four years older than I, but he was five grades ahead of me in school. This was because he entered the first grade when he was only five. When I began high school, I was the only Rapp child in attendance. The others were either in college, or had married. It was no longer feasible for my parents to maintain the apartment. Like my three oldest sisters, I lived with a family as an *au pair*.

The first family fired me because I hadn't kept the shades in my bedroom drawn at the same level, and my room faced the street. Also, I had taken a Kleenex from a box of tissues used for their infant. This was my first job away from home. When I realized the woman had asked to speak to Mama because she wanted to fire me, I sat down on the stairs and wept. The woman's seventy-five-year-old mother felt very compassionate towards me, and gave me a sewing basket as a present. I heard Mama say, "Well, I don't want my daughter staying here if that's the way you feel."

I went to work for another family. The wife had delusions of grandeur. I ate in the kitchen while the family was having dinner. If they wanted something, they rang a little bell to call me. I had always thought it sounded glamorous for a young girl to live away from home and work for another family. The family would either love her or hate her. Either way, it seemed glamorous. The reality, for me, was not.

During my sophomore and junior years, I worked for the Jewart family. I felt much better about the attitudes expressed towards me and the working conditions there. Everything was going along fine, until one evening when Mrs. Jewart came into my room and sat on the edge of my bed. She had just started taking a ceramics class. She told me she was going to love ceramics, but that there was this horrible woman in her class, Ida —, who kept interrupting the teacher and taking things without asking the owner. I was much too embarrassed to tell her the woman was my aunt.

This continued the rest of the year. She kept telling me about this awful woman. Every weekend, when I went home,

Mama asked me what her little sister had been up to to irritate Mrs. Jewart. Mama was amused by the whole situation.

Meanwhile, I lived a life of quiet desperation. If I was walking down the street with Mrs. Jewart, and I saw my Aunt Ida, I had to make an excuse and dash into a store. I was working on a family tree for my biology class that year. I had to keep it hidden under my bed. Once I had to hide it real fast when Mrs. Jewart came into my room. On another occasion, Mrs. Jewart had taken me up to the ranch to visit Mama. She seemed preoccupied with photographs of my cousin's high school pictures. They bore a striking resemblance to Aunt Ida. Fortunately she became preoccupied with a rose bush that was growing in through the window and lost her train of thought.

I lived with my friend Evelyn Kennet's family during my senior year. They treated me more like a daughter than a maid servant. They hoped I would set a good example for Evelyn, who was a little on the wild side. Her parents were constantly holding me up to her as an example. This made me uncomfortable.

I had an after school job that year, working in a bakery. I liked the job, and, for the first time, I had spending money of my own. But I regret that I didn't have more time to study in high school. We all found it necessary to work during high school, and then to help with the farm work on weekends. We had to grow up early!

THERE'S NO PLACE LIKE HOME (THE ROAD TRIP)

I ALWAYS WONDERED WHY Papa talked so funny. He said things like "arter" for ought to, "you all" for all of you, and "ruckus" for a confusing noise. (For example: "You all arter stop that ruckus.") Papa was very well read, particularly in history, geology, and astronomy. Despite the fact that they farmed the land all of their lives, the Rapps all loved to read. However, this inexplicable hick way of talking that Papa had became clear to me after our trip to Missouri.

The summer I turned twenty, Mama and Papa and I took an automobile trip to Missouri, Papa's childhood home. Mama was fifty-eight, and Papa was seventy-four. Papa had moved from Missouri to California at the age of thirty-three.

Papa wanted to make this road trip so much that he didn't tell anyone ahead of time he was feeling poorly. When he lay down on the back seat, shortly after we left, Mama commented, "This doesn't look so good." By the time we reached Sheridan Springs, Kansas, Papa was running a high fever. We stopped at a small motel and looked for a doctor. We told the owner of the motel we would be staying a few days, so our rent was lowered to two dollars a day.

Mama asked the motel owner if she could recommend a good doctor. The woman said, "Yes M'am, we have a fine feller who jest works miracles. He can fix anything. Yes siree. If he would jest quit workin' on them horses and cows and start dealin' with people, we would all be happy."

Mama snapped, "Do you have an M.D. in town? I want the letters 'M.D.' after his name."

The woman, looking dejected by this point, said, "Wal, all right now. If you insist," and gave us the name of

232

a medical doctor.

We needed a thermometer to take Papa's temperature. Kansas was a dry state, so not even medicinal alcohol could be obtained. I finally found a pharmacist who sold me a thermometer with a little alcohol inside the case. The local yokels followed our crisis with interest. As I returned to the motel, one of them hollered, "Did'ja get that alcohol?"

The doctor's daughter was graduating from high school that night. The doctor wanted to attend the ceremony and had very little time. His fee for an office visit was two dollars, but he asked four dollars for a motel call. He administered a shot of penicillin, at the time a fairly new drug.

Papa's temperature finally lowered. However, during the crisis, the motel owner tried to cheer us up by chirping, "Yes'm, that's how my husband went. Well one day, and dead the next."

When the crisis had passed, Mama and I collapsed with laughter.

PAPA RECOVERED and we continued on to Missouri. We stopped at the Morrison Place, his home for thirty-three years. We met many of his friends and relatives. I found myself fascinated by their speech, which sounded just like Papa's.

I remember they spoke of chivarees, a Southern term for when boys would serenade girls at night. The young man generally played a ukelele, a banjo, drums or anything else that would make noise, and sang to his lady love. Frequently, they said, the girl's father had to throw something at them to finally make them stop.

Martin and Theodore Bertsch were doubly related to Papa. Their mother was Papa's cousin on his father's side. She married his mother's brother. So she was Papa's cousin by birth, and his aunt by marriage. Her children were Papa's first *and* second cousins. Since their mother was much older than Papa, he had always called her Aunt Helen.

Theodore had chickens throughout his farmhouse. Since he was a bachelor, Kate, Martin's wife, prepared the meal. We had chicken, biscuits and gravy, salad fresh from the garden, and homemade strawberry shortcake.

I met Belle Crigler Knowles, whom Uncle Louis had been so much in love with many years earlier. We had dinner with her. She was a charming, gracious hostess.

Papa's first grade teacher, a vivacious woman with snow white hair and silky smooth skin, was eighty-nine when I met her. She began teaching at fifteen in the little one room school house. She offered me a coke. I remember thinking she was really "with it."

Mama and I wanted to see the cemetery where Papa's parents were buried. We crossed a field as a shortcut. I looked to my right and, less than twenty feet away, saw a large bull swishing his tail and keeping a steady eye on our passing. I wanted to run. Mama, sensing this, said, "Just keep walking, Margaret, don't you run." We made it across the field successfully. We entered the cemetery as guests, rather than as permanent residents.

THE TRIP HOME proved as adventurous as the trip east had been. Papa's cousin Martin and his wife Kate came with us. This was their first trip to California. Our 1940 Chevrolet was crowded. Martin and Kate were inexperienced travelers. Martin worried about his corn crop. They fussed constantly.

We took the southern route to show them Las Vegas and Los Angeles. It was hot. You haven't known hot until you've crossed Nevada in July without air conditioning. We rented a couple of motel rooms in Las Vegas and were in bed by eight o'clock.

Papa wanted to get an early start to avoid the mid-day heat. He decided upon four in the morning. During the night, Papa woke and asked me the time. I opened one eye and looked at my watch. "Ten minutes to four." Papa woke everyone up and told them to get ready.

Once I looked at my watch, I realized my error. It was really only ten o'clock. We had only slept two hours. However, I was too embarrassed to admit my mistake.

Driving through Las Vegas, we noticed the casinos filled with people. Mama, who thought it was five o'clock in the morning by now, said, "Boy, Adolph, they never go to bed

Aunt Helen in Missouri. She was a first cousin of Adolph Rapp, Sr. by birth, who married an uncle of his by marriage. She immigrated from Germany in 1867. Photo c. 1920s.

in this town!"

We continued on our journey with everyone, except me, expecting the sun to rise at any moment. Martin said, "The cocks ain't gonna crow this morning, are they, Adolph?"

It was still dark when we arrived at the California stateline two hours later. We stopped to stretch. Mama asked, "Now just exactly what time is it, Margaret?" I told her it was one o'clock. Because of her exhaustion, she was furious. All she could say was, "Oh Margaret, what have you done?"

Mama fell asleep at the wheel going over Cajon Pass. Martin saw her dozing, but he was an extremely timid man. He began to right the steering wheel. Mama was startled and grasped the wheel. As the car continued to move toward the edge of the road adjoining the steep cliff, it hit a trailer filled with food. It belonged to a Mexican family entering California to harvest fruit. The family had brought a large supply of food with them, as this was during wartime rationing. Purchasing food in California would have been difficult for them.

Mama promptly fainted. The father of the Mexican family began screaming in Spanish, *"Caramba!"* One of the daughters spoke English and she and I exchanged addresses.

We were towed to Barstow, California, and spent the Fourth of July weekend there.

After this, no one was feeling very well. On my twentieth birthday, we drove up the coastal highway to show Martin and Kate the spectacular scenery. However, since they were frequently car sick, I drove the five hundred miles home without stopping to see any sights.

I will never forget that day. Martin and Kate were obviously wishing they had never left Missouri. Mama, Papa and I were all eager to get back to the Santa Cruz Mountains. I guess the saying is true: "There's no place like home."

PAPA CONTINUED TO CORRESPOND with his friends in Missouri. One of them, Carl Robinson, a boyhood friend of Papa's that I met when we were back there, wrote Papa this letter many years after our road trip:

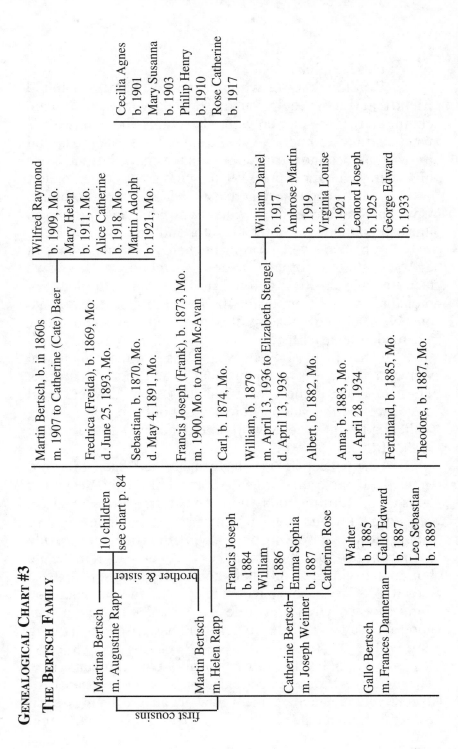

GENEALOGICAL CHART #3
THE BERTSCH FAMILY

Martina Bertsch
m. Augustine Rapp

10 children
see chart p. 84

brother & sister

first cousins

Martin Bertsch
m. Helen Rapp

Francis Joseph
b. 1884
William
b. 1886

Catherine Bertsch
m. Joseph Weimer

Emma Sophia
b. 1887
Catherine Rose

Gallo Bertsch
m. Frances Danneman

Walter
b. 1885
Gallo Edward
b. 1887
Leo Sebastian
b. 1889

Martin Bertsch, b. in 1860s
m. 1907 to Catherine (Cate) Baer

Fredrica (Freida), b. 1869, Mo.
d. June 25, 1893, Mo.

Sebastian, b. 1870, Mo.
d. May 4, 1891, Mo.

Francis Joseph (Frank), b. 1873, Mo.
m. 1900, Mo. to Anna McAvan

Carl, b. 1874, Mo.

William, b. 1879
m. April 13, 1936 to Elizabeth Stengel
d. April 13, 1936

Albert, b. 1882, Mo.

Anna, b. 1883, Mo.
d. April 28, 1934

Ferdinand, b. 1885, Mo.

Theodore, b. 1887, Mo.

Wilfred Raymond
b. 1909, Mo.
Mary Helen
b. 1911, Mo.
Alice Catherine
b. 1918, Mo.
Martin Adolph
b. 1921, Mo.

Cecilia Agnes
b. 1901
Mary Susanna
b. 1903
Philip Henry
b. 1910
Rose Catherine
b. 1917

William Daniel
b. 1917
Ambrose Martin
b. 1919
Virginia Louise
b. 1921
Leonord Joseph
b. 1925
George Edward
b. 1933

April 7, 1963

Dear Adolph,

Don't look to see who this letter is from. Just an old friend that yous't to help you thresh wheat with the old steam engine and a thirty man crew. The best thing about those days was those good dinners we would have. Those beef roast and brown potatoes and the trimmings that went with it and those blackberry and apple pies. What a change has been made.

In '61 I had fifteen acres of wheat. I hired a combine. It was a good day and the wheat was good and dry and in thirteen hours it was in the elevator and I had 540 bushels.

When you were farming out here 25 bushels of wheat and 50 bushels of corn to the acre was a good yield. Now we use time and fertiliser and hybrid seed and with plenty of moisture, we can produce 40 bushels of wheat and 90 bushels of corn to the acre. Research and better know how has made the difference.

It has been eighteen years this summer when you were out here. I was flat on my back in bed and 60 years old. That fall I went to the Vocal Clinic in Kansas City and from there I went to the Mayo Clinic. I was 'bout two years getting well. I had eight years of work left in me and I got a lot done in that time....

I help keep house, have a garden, keep the yard mowed. I believe alike work is for me. I like to tell the young boys that is farming today how we cut the corn with a fifty cent corn knife and shuck it with a fifteen cent peg, how we would plow with walking plows, work the young mules, ride to town horeseback, get ice in the winter and put it in the ice box in the summer. I tell them how everything was done in those days—try to smear it on thick just to find out what they think. Don't say but very little. They look at me and just as good as to say you are the biggest liar I have lisent to in a long time.....

Adolph, I want to write you about our cemetary here. Those of us who are concerned about the poor prospects of decent maintenance in the years ahead are trying to do something about it. Our idea is to establish a perpetual endowment to care for it in the years ahead. The necessary legal instruments would be drawn to provide for our association and trust fund. Do you remember Mr. Bill Nivat? His grandson is our attorney...I am receiving a favorable response to all of my letters. We have our quotes about made and we will appreciate a donation little or big if you are interested. Plias make check to Pleasant Cemetary for endowment....

It has been eighteen years since you were out here. Don't you feel you could make the trip back? Well, Lee and I are going to envite you and Mrs. Rapp to make a visit this summer. It is a short trip now days. Take a jet and be in Kansas City three and a half hours. We can meet you there and three and a half more hours we will have you out here on your stompin' groun.

I would like for you to see what change has been made. The state built a new road from the Sam Broun place to the Huricane Bridge seventy feet wide and made the country look a lot different. We also have a new rode from Old Church to Crossroads school house. You will remember that road. That is where the horse ran away with you and Bill Baars....

I want to write you about our weather. We had a cold winter, ten and twelve below zero. The river had ice in it all winter and the river was low when it froze over and was blocked for three weeks. When it broke up there was piles of ice four and five feet high on the bank and look to be twelve inches thick. Today we are having 70 degree weather.

Now Lee and I will be looking for yew this summer— bring Mrs. Rapp with you and we'll have a good visit. Hello to all the family I have seen.

Good health and happy days.

> Yours,
> Carl Robinson

Papa never did return to Missouri. The road trip we made in 1946 was the last time he ever saw his childhood home.

Mama's Driving

THE ACCIDENT ON CAJON PASS was the only really serious one Mama ever had, and I was partially to blame that time. After all, if I hadn't gotten the time wrong, she wouldn't have been asleep at the wheel. However, Mama's driving did leave a little bit to be desired.

Mama learned to drive when she was thirty-four. Three years later, Papa gave up the driver's seat. Mama never did have much faith in the automobile's dependability, either. This new invention hadn't been popular in the mountains when she was growing up. Whenever we got within two miles of home, she would say, "Well, we could walk it now."

Her driving tended to be cautious. Her speed was five miles an hour on the winding mountain roads. I'm sure this saved her life on occasion. It also saved Frank from serious injury, or worse, the time he fell out the back seat of the Maxwell. I remember Mama telling Papa once, "You know that Belle is getting to be a really wild driver. On the open road, she was doing thirty-five miles an hour!"

Though a cautious driver, she was not the safest driver. When approaching a freeway, no matter how busy it was, she would let three cars go by. Then she would turn into traffic, saying, "They've got to let you in!" She blasted her horn throughout this maneuver, barging right onto the freeway. I remember praying a lot.

Once, when my nephew Joe Callaghan was riding with her, she cut the corner a little too close and went up over the curb. Pedestrians were jumping out of her way. Her comment was, "They're always putting things in the way!"

MAMA QUITE LITERALLY BUMPED INTO Dr. Picchi in Oakland. Mama and Papa were on their way to my Brother Frank's

Mama pulled a real cliff hanger on Margaret's wedding day.

house. Papa tended to be a back seat driver, and this annoyed Mama. She claimed she knew the traffic light was red, but was teaching Papa a lesson. He told her to go ahead. She didn't see any cars at the intersection, so she figured the worst thing that would happen would be that they'd get a traffic ticket.

But city drivers drove faster than mountain drivers. Mama jumped out of her car as soon as she bumped into Dr. Picchi's car. She ran over to him, flustered and excited, full of apologies. When she found out the young man was a doctor, she explained that she and her husband were just on their way to visit their son, who was also a doctor.

Dr. Picchi and my brother Frank had never met. But they were both about the same age, both lived in Oakland, and they shared the same profession. As a result of this accident, the two became fast friends. Their families are still on friendly terms today.

FOLLOWING MY WEDDING IN CAPITOLA, Mama drove my husband and me to the reception being held at the ranch in the mountains. That time she said there was too much play in the steering wheel. Whatever the cause, she drove over a cliff, and we were left hanging on by two wheels.

From the back seat, I helped Mama open her car door. This was a two door car. Only the one on Mama's side was accessible for exit. First Mama got out, then Papa got out, then I got out, then the cake got out, and finally my new husband got out. (My husband, who had the cake sitting on his lap, handed it to me before escaping from the perilous vehicle.)

To the worry of many, Mama drove until she was seventy-seven years old.

TWILIGHT TIME

THANKSGIVING 1965, Mama looked around the table and said, "Well, I've almost got my family raised. They're all in their forties and fifties." (Actually, I was not quite forty.)

Mama spoke of her children as her investment, and her grandchildren as her dividends. Her investments provided her with a high yield. Among the eight children she bore, she had lost only one, who was stillborn. By 1965, she had twenty-three grandchildren and five great-grandchildren.

Mama felt it had been a privilege to be poor because she could better appreciate what she had later in life. She said it was better to pursue than to possess. This was some of Mama's homespun philosophy.

Mama attended the 1915 World's Fair in San Francisco, where Thomas Edison, Henry Ford, Luther Burbank and Harvey Firestone were all in attendance. She said they were grand old gentleman. During her lifetime, she witnessed the arrival of electricity, telephone service, radio, television, airplanes, and the advent of the NASA space program.

"Education, communication, transportation," she used to chant. "Those are the three big changes I saw in my lifetime."

Mama was able to vote in the first election when American women won voting privileges. She was an early feminist, and always encouraged her daughters to go as far as they could with their education and their careers. She taught me to read and write before I began grammar school.

ON APRIL 1, 1966, Mama was out hoeing weeds and preparing the garden for early spring planting. She was almost seventy-seven years old. Papa came out and said, "You know Emma, you ain't no spring chicken anymore. You aren't to be working so hard." He proceeded to help her with the hoeing.

Papa was fascinated with the show "Death Valley Days," and he watched it that night before going to bed. (He had listened to the radio show long before it was on television.) Papa had never been to Death Valley himself. My family and I were planning to start on a road trip to Death Valley the next morning, and I imagine the thought of us starting on this trip must have crossed his mind during the program.

Upon going to bed that night, he took Mama a glass of lemonade. He complained that he had not been able to see the picture on the television very well. His eyesight had been failing for some time, but that night it was particularly bad.

About two o'clock in the morning, Mama felt Papa stiffen. She heard his breathing stop. She lay there beside him through the night, as he grew cold.

I got a call from her at seven o'clock the next morning. She said, "Margaret dear, I hate to startle you, but I think your father might be starting to go." I reacted, and then she said, "In fact, I hate to have to tell you dear, but he is gone."

Mama said she could have felt guilty for allowing Papa to help with the hoeing the previous day. After all, he was ninety-four. But she knew he had gone suddenly, and peacefully. Mama and Papa had been married for fifty-eight years.

Mama grieved quietly. She once said to me, "You know Margaret, I could get hysterical and cry and scream. But at my age, I can't afford that luxury. I have to get through one day at a time."

Mama disliked sensationalism—particularly with regard to funerals. If she saw someone wailing and moaning over a loved one, she would say, "They are trying to ease a guilty conscience for not caring enough for that person when they were alive." She thought it was much better to show love and respect for the living rather to than to grieve at a funeral so openly.

Mama was hesitant to enter her bedroom the night after Papa died, so Emma Mae promised to stay with her until she composed herself. But once they finally entered the room, Mama started talking at random, recounting familiar stories, reliving their lives together. She strung thoughts together, like pearls on a necklace. She reminisced about their courtship and marriage, the births of their children, the Blabon Place, the Crane Place, the history of the Crane Place, Skyland Church, their faith. She spoke about the early mountain folks, their births, weddings, and deaths. She said she would like to see a home on the hill (at the Crane Place) for retired priests. Although she had been Presbyterian all of her life, she said she would like to see Papa have a real Catholic funeral, one that would have pleased his mother. She mentioned that Papa had just bought some tomato plants for his garden, and that she wanted to plant them for him. She said again and again how she would like to write a book about the Santa Cruz Mountains and the people she had known there, preserving their stories for posterity.

She told Emma Mae, "Papa made my life happy. If I cry, I am crying for Emma."

MAMA KEPT HERSELF OCCUPIED over the next several years by straightening out her affairs, and organizing her papers and momentos.

During this period, she fulfilled her lifelong dream of going to Alaska. Her granddaughter Patsy went with her. Many years earlier, she and Mrs. Parker had planned to go, but Captain Parker had vetoed the idea.

Mama started giving away many of her photos and memorabilia. It was very important for her to know that each item went to the person she thought would most appreciate it.

Mama obtained an address in San Francisco for her niece Alice, her sister Alvina's daughter who had been orphaned at an early age. Mama hadn't seen Alice in over fifty years. Ten years previously, Alice had written Mama a very bitter letter saying, "The Ingraham sisters pruned me out of the family tree years ago, and I ain't gonna be grafted back on now."

Mama felt that Alice should have the picture of her own mother that graced the mantel in the Big Room for as long as I could remember. So Mama mailed it to her.

A few months later, a strange woman drove up the long driveway. She came to the kitchen door and shoved a package into Mama's hands. Mama asked, "What is it?" The woman said, "Open it and find out." She marched right back to her car and drove off, without saying another word. When Mama opened the package, she found the picture of Alvina. She had not recognized the woman. But many years had passed since she had seen Alice.

Mama received this letter from Alice in 1965:

Mrs. Emma Rapp,

Again it is that time of year when Thanksgiving dinner is foremost in everyone's mind—And as I reminisce I find the most memorable Thanksgiving dinner in my life was one spent in your father's home at Skyland—the year 1918, the day November 28th.

My dinner consisted of one five cent can of sardines and six soda crackers counted out for me—my dinner was due to the lies you told. The family all ate turkey and all the trimmings at your table. Just want you to understand that I have not forgotten you nor your HATE.

Alice Alvina

I never discovered what lies she was accusing Mama of, or what the cause of their feud had been. But apparently Alice had carried this grudge for forty-seven years.

THE LAST STORY

THIS BOOK IS PRIMARILY A COLLECTION of stories Mama told me over a period of fifty years. However, she wasn't able to tell me the last story. So I will tell it as best I can.

The last week of her life, Mama began to look her age and talk of dying. The last time she spoke with my husband Amadeus, whom she adored, she said, "I don't know what I'm hanging around for anymore. I'm just taking up space and I have collected so many things that won't be of value to anyone. They'll probably just have one big bonfire after I'm gone."

August 9, 1975 would have been Mama's eighty-seventh birthday. We were planning a party at our home to which we had invited the entire family.

Mama had recently stepped up her efforts to give her momentos and old photos to whomever she felt would best appreciate them. I was at the ranch that August fourth, and so was my sister Mary. Mama tried to get me to take a whole box of photos she had sorted out just for me. At that very moment, I looked at the clock and noticed how late it was. I said to Mama, "I can get them when I come and pick you up for your birthday party on Saturday. I will pick you up Friday." She looked so disappointed. I've always regretted not taking those pictures with me.

On August seventh, I made plans to spend the night at our trailer which we had parked in The Willows, (half a mile from the ranch.) The weather had been incredibly hot, and I had been working hard all week on the party plans. I told my husband I needed a break. I was picking Mama up the next day, anyway.

As I passed through Los Gatos, I stopped at an outside

teller of the Bank of America. My mind froze as I saw the date on the window, August eighth. If this was correct, Mama's party was the next day. I had to pick her up and take her back to my place. I had much too much to do to spend the night at The Willows relaxing. One of the other customers assured me that it was a mistake. It was really August seventh.

THE NEXT MORNING, I was relaxing by the pool when my husband called. He said, "Mama wants to know when you're going to get there." I told him I would be leaving in just a few minutes. Then the owner of The Willows asked, "Margaret, if you're not in a hurry, could you watch the snack bar for me while I get a bite to eat?" I told her I wasn't in a hurry.

When she came back, I drove the short distance to the ranch. I'll never know why I parked at the bottom of the road. There was a long winding driveway, about a quarter of a mile up the hill. We usually only parked at the bottom by the mailbox in the redwood grove if the road was muddy. This wouldn't have been the case on that hot, dry August day.

I felt relaxed and at peace as I walked slowly up the steep hill. About half way up, I started to hear a loud crackling sound, and to smell smoke. I broke into a run.

I ran up the cement steps of the north porch and all through the house, but I couldn't find Mama anywhere. The house was not on fire, but all of the outbuildings and the orchard were. The fire was moving towards the madrone grove, and the house. I didn't think to call the fire department. I called my husband in San Jose, and told him to hurry up and get there, because the ranch was on fire. He asked me where Mama was. I said, "I don't know. I've looked all through the house and I don't see her anywhere." My husband said he couldn't leave right away since our son Ken had the car.

The house was completely deserted. Our son Doug had been living there for a couple of years. Mama's sixteen-year-old great-granddaughter Donna was also visiting her at the time. But I couldn't find either of them.

I ran to the cottage to look for the hose to put out the fire, which was raging by this time. Some of the neighbors had phoned the fire department, and the fire had been spotted from the lookout point on top of Loma Prieta. Fire Ranger helicopters were circling over the orchard. I thought, "Oh no, my car is blocking the driveway."

I ran down and moved my car just in time. When I entered the house again, through the kitchen door this time, which was the one we usually used, I noticed a whole stack of Mama's unopened birthday cards on the table. They had just come in the mail that day, and she had not had time to read them yet.

John Rosenberg, the owner of The Willows, appeared at the door and asked where my mother was. I was numb by this time. I said, "Oh, I don't know. She either went to town with Doug, or she's out in the fire." He went out to look for her. Several other neighbors had arrived by this time. I passed from the kitchen through the cloak room and saw Mama's purse hanging on the coat hook. That's when I knew she hadn't gone to town.

John Rosenberg came back and said, "You were right, Margaret, your mother is out there. Don't come out." He drove me the mile over to his house, which was right next to The Willows.

Like a blurry dream, I remember seeing the coroner's car pass us on its way up to the ranch, and again on its way back down. It was Mama's last trip out of the mountains that she loved so dearly.

My husband and Ken picked me up that afternoon, and we went back to the ranch. Donna had returned from Santa Cruz bearing gifts for her great-grandmother. She was hysterical when she saw the remains from the fire and heard about Mama. She screamed, "The house is haunted! Great-grandfather is here!" I said if he was, it was wonderful, because he was a very special man.

I called all of the other family members and told them the awful news. They thought I might be calling about some last minute plans for Mama's birthday party, so these were difficult calls to make.

My brother Frank was particularly upset when he heard how she died. He said burning is one of the worst

Mama and Papa pose with nineteen of their twenty-three grandchildren, on their golden anniversary, 1958. Back row l. to r.: Audrey Clausen, Joe Callaghan, Papa, Mama, David Rapp, Leo Rapp. Second row l. to r.: Danny Kitzmiller, Louis Rapp, Susan Kitzmiller, Larry Tarquinio, Michael Lydon (behind Susan and Larry), Doug Tarquinio, Meg Rapp, Patsy Rapp, Carl Kitzmiller. Front row l. to r.: Ken Tarquinio, Steve Tarquinio, Mary Lydon, Maure Rapp, Terese Rapp, Kathy Rapp. Agnes Rapp was a nun at this time, and unable to attend. Three grandchildren were not yet born: Frank Kitzmiller, Francine Rapp and Janet Tarquinio.

possible ways to go.

BECAUSE SHE WAS ONE OF THE LAST MATRIARCHS in the Santa Cruz Mountains, and because of the awful circumstances of her death, it was on all the local news programs that night. Many people who had known the family in the past heard of her death in that way.

My niece Audrey said a woman came into her flower shop in Vallejo and asked her if she had heard about the horrible death of the old woman in the Santa Cruz Mountains. Audrey said, "She was my grandmother."

Mary had ordered a large birthday cake from the bakery. At the last minute, she had the decorations changed to a cross and lilies.

My daughter Janet was eleven years old at the time. She was arriving home from summer camp the next day. She expected someone to meet her. She wondered why she was kept waiting so long, and why no one answered when she phoned home. We were supposed to be having a big birthday party, and she thought maybe no one heard the phone. Ken finally picked her up. She asked him why they were heading in the wrong direction. They stopped to get gas, and Ken told her they were going to the ranch because grandma had died.

I was twelve when I had my first real experience with death, so I could understand her feelings. I still remember my daughter's ashen face when they arrived at the ranch. Much of the grounds were decimated by the fire, and the place felt deserted, dead.

THE AUTOPSY REVEALED that Mama hadn't inhaled any smoke into her lungs. They said she must have died instantly, probably from a heart attack.

Mama used to burn her garbage in the incinerator. In those days, there was no garbage pick up for people in the Santa Cruz Mountains. So Mama burned her trash each day. The heart attack must have occurred just as she was lighting a match. Although the fire fanned out, devastating a large area, the papers in the incinerator had not burned. Mamas body, lying next to it, was partially burned.

The fire blazed a trail from her body straight up the hill to Sammy's unmarked grave. I learned this six months later from my sister Elizabeth. She was present when Papa buried Mama's stillborn baby, and it was she who had shown Mama the grave site years later. Mama did not ask Elizabeth to show her the grave site until after Papa had died.

ALL OF MAMA'S FAVORITE HYMNS from her years as the church pianist were played at her funeral: "What a Friend We Have in Jesus," "The Old Rugged Cross," "Amazing Grace."

Our son Steve was travelling through Alaska at the time of Mama's death. We knew he couldn't make it home for the funeral, so we chose not to notify him until he got back. He returned the following week. We didn't say anything about it during dinner. After everyone went to bed, I stayed up with him to tell him. That's when he said, "Mom, I know about Grandma."

He had hitched a ride up to the ranch before coming home. He wanted to visit his grandmother first. He was tired and dusty and he wanted to wash up. He knew immediately what had happened when he saw the house boarded up and the devastation from the fire. Mama had never locked a door in all her sixty years in that home. He told the woman who had given him a ride, "My grandmother died." The woman felt so sorry for him, she gave him a ride all the way back to our home in San Jose.

Several months after Mama died, I learned why Donna had been afraid of the haunted house, and why she was so convinced my father was there that day. Mama had told her that morning, "You know, Donna dear, your great-grandfather is going to come visit me today."

So maybe Mama did tell the last story, after all.

APPENDICES

NOTES AND SOURCES

The primary source for the stories and legends in this book was Emma Bessie Ingraham Rapp. Although she died in 1975, she was such a prolific and colorful raconteur that many people still retell her stories to their children, grandchildren and friends. As much as possible, we have tried to preserve the spirit of her vision of the pioneer days in the Santa Cruz Mountains.

Where we felt it was essential to round out our book with a few facts culled from other sources, we first consulted long-time mountain residents who remembered characters and events from the Skyland area and environs early in this century. We will cite these people below under the chapter title where the relevant story or information appears. You may assume that anything which is not cited either here or at the place where it is first mentioned is attributable to Emma Rapp.

In a few instances we have used facts and stories conned from the pages of other historical books, especially in the chapters on the Santa Cruz Mountains and Skyland before the turn of the century. A selected bibliography is as follows:

Ghost Towns of the Santa Cruz Mountains, by John V. Young, Western Tanager Press, 1984.

The Howling Wilderness: The Summit Road of the Santa Cruz Mountains 1850-1906, by Stephen Payne, California History Center, De Anza College, 1978.

Out West, by Mike Flanagan, Harry N. Abrams, Inc. Publishers, 1987.

These books are among the best loved in our family library. However, we hope this book will bring something new to historical publications on the Santa Cruz Mountains—the stories of many, many early settlers who have not yet been recorded in the books mentioned above, or in any other book of this type. We intentionally did not focus on the big land owners, lumber barons and local celebrities. These more familiar characters form the backdrop of our book. Instead, we focused on the farmers, the teachers, the mid-wives, the preachers, the traveling salesmen and the children.

The following is more than a list of sources. It also includes a few more juicy tales to round out your reading experience. Although most of the chapters are listed here, the few chapters which are obviously based entirely on Emma Rapp's tales and the author's personal experiences do not appear here.

THE CRANE PLACE

The succession of ownership of the Longridge Road property within the Crane family was determined through deeds filed with the Santa Cruz County Recorder's Office. The property was traced all the way back to the original U.S. Patent legitimizing the original Mexican land grant which created Rancho San Vicente, later known to Americans who lived in the area as "Spanish Ranch."

Stanley Fidel told us about his family's winery. He also told us that the Cranes were frequently cited in the books. The quote about the Fidel winery operating in Skyland, "despite the fact that Skyland is of a temperance order," is from J.J. Bamber's publication *The Realty*. As mentioned elsewhere in this book, this was really more of a news sheet listing properties for sale, and including a few tidbits of local gossip. None of the residents who remember the Skyland area during the early part of this century ever mention an instance when one of the local wineries or stills ever ran into any trouble during prohibition. Perhaps because the area was so isolated, they had fewer problems with the Feds than their counterparts in town.

DESTINATION: WRIGHT'S

This is, without a doubt, the chapter which is most dependant on secondary sources. Most of the mountain residents referred to throughout the rest of this book moved to the area around the turn of the century. However, since the region was settled only half a century earlier, we thought we would quickly sketch this history

The fascinating stories about the two Charley's are best told by John Young in his *Ghost Tales of the Santa Cruz Mountains*. Young had the advantage of writing these stories more than half a century ago, so he was just as close to his oldest tales in 1934 as we are in 1995 to ours. His book was originally published as a series of articles in the *San Jose Mercury Herald*.

The summary of prominent early pioneer families of the last century is derived from information in Stephen Paine's *The Howling Wilderness*. Paine goes into much greater detail about the fortunes of these families, as his book focuses on the Summit area leading up to the year 1906.

Wright's Rifle Club, and its founder John Utschcig, are mentioned in both Young's and Paine's books. The importance of Wright's was well understood by all of the early mountain residents, as it was their primary link to the outside world. Many of the people mentioned in this book first arrived in the mountains by taking the train to Wright's, and the mail for mountain residents came through Wright's station. The date that service commenced, May 15, 1880, was obtained from Paine's book. Some sources put the date train service ended to Wright's a little later. However our date is based on a letter Brother received postmarked Los Gatos, rather than Wright's.

The Miltonmont is still standing today, although it is now a private residence. We pass by it almost every day on our way to town. The Willows is also still operational, although it is currently a residential trailer park. Paine and

Young both recorded the information that Donald Beadel originally purchased the land for The Willows from lumber lord Frederic A. Hihn. The fact that Beadel's son Alex built the famous indoor swimming pool also comes from them. However, the pool was still there during the author's childhood, and it was well known to her.

The story of Frederick Hihn, who landed with nothing but his pack on his back and built a lumber empire, is from Young. The facts about the lumber industry—who owned what and where—are from *The Howling Wilderness*. The information about the fruit industry in the Santa Cruz Mountains was well known to the author and most of the sources cited in this book, as it was their business.

The biographical information on the Fidel's is from Eloise Fidel Adams. Stanley Fidel first mentioned the family winery to us.

It is true that the fruit grown in the Santa Cruz Mountains was famous for being so sweet during the heyday of this industry. In fact once, Captain John Parker, who owned The Willows at the time, was nibbling on some grapes in a produce market in San Francisco when he noticed how remarkably good they were. He said to his wife Delphine, "These are so sweet, they taste like they came from the Santa Cruz Mountains." When he read the label on the crate, it said "A. Rapp, Wrights, California."

GO WEST YOUNG MAN

The dates when Joseph Ingraham joined the Northern Army, and when he died, are recorded on his discharge papers. The rest is family legend.

THE INGRAHAM FAMILY

The primary source for the tragic story of Bert

Ingraham's suicide is Eloise Fidel Adams. She was an eye witness, as she was actually home when Johnny Wood came bursting into their place to say that Bert had chased him away with Wood's own gun. Others are still alive who remember Bert's suicide. However, all of the details of this story from the time that Bert leaves his mother's room are directly from Eloise; and as far as we know, she is the only living person who would remember this part of the event. The dates of his death and burial were obtained from the coroner's report, as was the language quoted from that report.

This seems like a good opportunity to clear up some earlier misinformation. In the obituaries for both Adolph and Emma Rapp, it states that the three Rapp brothers founded the Mountain Telephone Company. However it was Hiram Ingraham who strung the first phone lines between his stores at Skyland and Burrell, and the first phone system in the mountains was operated from his General Store at Burrell. It is very possible that the Rapp brothers helped extend this system; however, it is equally possible that thirty years ago a reporter confused Emma's father with her husband, and Adolph Rapp has been geting the credit instead of Hiram Ingraham ever since.

SKYLAND

Eloise Fidel Adams told us the story of Helen McEwen's donation of a church bell to the Skyland Church. This fact has been noted in other publications, however she had more to say about it.

THE VON RAPP FAMILY

For the information that the von Rapps left Germany to escape the horrors of the Franco-Prussian War, we have Ruth and Esther Jaun to thank. They have put exhaustive efforts into researching the Rapp family.

Adolph Rapp, Sr. always said his family's name was originally von Rapp, and that they dropped the "von" when they moved to the new country so the name would sound less German. It is not known if he knew that the German "von" is similar to "sir" in England. The history of the von Rapps in Germany, including when and how they picked up this title is unknown.

Family legend has it that Louis failed to win any land in the Cherokee Strip Race, when the U.S. government was giving away most of the state of Oklahoma, while the Suter boy was successful and settled in Oklahoma. Basic facts about the "Oklahoma Sooners," including the story about the man who said he raised his vegetables in ten minutes, were obtained from *Out West*, by Mike Flanagan.

The story about Aunt Kate and Uncle Will winning a car is well known to many people; however, Eloise Fidel said Will Baars won it by selling magazine subscriptions, and that he had to buy many of those himself. Another version of this story holds that he bought raffle tickets.

The story of Rena Rapp and Chris Jaun's courtship and marriage was told to us by Ruth Jaun.

TURN OF THE CENTURY VIGNETTES

The first two vignettes, "The Baritone" and "The Unwanted Suitor," were told by Phyllis Griner, Belle Ingraham Griner's daughter. Roger Mason told us the second vignette, about his great-grandfather Clayton Jones. Eloise Fidel Adams recounted the story of Bill and Anna Marie Adams' unusual wedding ceremony. The Adams were her in-laws.

SALVADORE

No attempt has been made to verify Salvadore's stories about being imprisoned in England or shipwrecked in a doomed ship off of the Chilean coast. However the author wished it to be known that she never knew Salvadore to lie.

The other stories about Salvadore's experiences in the Santa Cruz Mountains are more or less direct from the people who lived those experiences with him.

LAUREL

Brother, who now goes by Adolph Rapp, still resides in the Santa Cruz Mountains after spending the entire seventy-eight years of his life there. He told us about how Mama got her groceries in the mail. This was an ingenious agreement between Mama, George Napier and her brother-in-law Will Hurney. This service lapsed after the train stopped running and Highway 17 opened up. As Adolph said, "Sometimes progress isn't progress." He also told us about how Mr. Napier carried families through the depression.

EMMA MAE REMEMBERS THE 1910s

The information on the Wragg family is from Marion Wragg Harris.

HOLY CITY

The facts of Riker's "Holy City" have been well documented; however this chapter is interesting because the author brings to it a depth of personal memories connected with this unusual "religious colony."

On an interesting side note, Tom Stanton, the founder of Holy City Art Glass, said he discovered a lot of Riker's original hate literature in a closet when he was preparing to open his glass shop in one of the colony's few remaining buildings.

Everyone's Crazy but Me and Thee...

Stanley Fidel told the story about the second explanation for Alice Benninghoven's conversion. The biographical information for "Mother" Alice, as well as the information about the two books she published, was discovered at UCSC Special Collections.

Best Friends

Some of the information in the footnote concerning Jack London and the other notables who spent time in the vicinity of White Wash Alley is from *The Howling Wilderness*. However, Emma Ingraham did mention the artists' bohemia up around White Wash Alley on several occasions, and she specifically mentioned Jack London and Ambrose Bierce in connection with it.

Many of the people in the mountains were not too fond of the Roosevelts, as evidenced by Mrs. Parker's letter. Emma Ingraham's opinion of Eleanor Roosevelt did change over the years though. In her later years, she admired Eleanor Roosevelt for her many good works.

School Days

Clara Rapp Clausen provided the information about Mama's involvement with the school board, and the rule enacted after Mrs. Eggleston was hired. She also told about how Frankie cried in order to get into the first grade when he was five years old.

There's No Place Like Home (The Road Trip)

Ruth Jaun provided us with the parish records from

Salisbury, Missouri for the latter part of the nineteenth century and the first part of this century. That aided us in determining the Bertsch family tree, as well as their relationship with the Rapp family.

INDEX

GENEALOGICAL CHART #4A

DESCENDANTS OF ADOLPH AND EMMA RAPP

Adolph Rapp
b. Sept. 28, 1871
Prairie Hill Missouri
d. April 2, 1966
Santa Cruz Mountains

m. Dec. 29, 1908

Emma Bessie Ingraham
b. Aug. 9, 1888
Kansas
D. Aug. 8, 1975
Santa Cruz Mountains

Elizabeth Martina—m. Nov. 30, 1929—John Joseph (Jack) Callaghan
b. Nov. 11, 1909
b. Canada
d. 1970

Emma Mae
b. June 12, 1911 — m. Aug. 19, 1939 — Robert Lydon
b. Jan. 10, 1909
d. Sept. 25, 1992

Clara Belle
b. July 11, 1915 — m. May 28, 1940 — Gorm Christian Clausen
d. June 20, 1990
b. Aug. 25, 1904, Marsta, Denmark
d. Jan. 27, 1958

Adolphus
b. Oct. 28, 1916 — m. July 10, 1938 — Lorene White
b. Aug. 9, 1913
d. Sept. 1, 1993

Mary Pearl
b. May 25, 1918 — m. Aug. 26, 1945 — Owen Kitzmiller
d. Feb. 14, 1981
b. Nov. 5, 1917, Texas
d. Jan. 6, 1982

Frank Everett
b. June 7, 1922 — m. Oct. 21, 1944 — Patricia Wheatcraft
d. April 2, 1995
b. Aug. 9, 1922

Sammy, stillborn

Margaret Louise — m. June 19, 1947 — Amadeus Constantine Tarquinio
b. July 9, 1926
b. Feb. 2, 1924, Jeannette, Pennsylvania
d. Oct. 19, 1994
d. April 19, 1995

GENEALOGICAL CHART #4B
DESCENDANTS OF ADOLPH AND EMMA RAPP

THE CALLAGHAN BRANCH

Elizabeth Rapp
m. Jack Callaghan

- John Joseph (Joe)
  b. April 20, 1932
  d. June 21, 1994
  m. Phyllis
  m. Carole
  (no issue)

  - Karen Elizabeth
    b. Jan. 5, 1954
    m. March 2, 1974
    to Richard Alan Hannegan
    - Allison Marie
      b. Aug. 6, 1977
    - Richard Casey
      b. Oct. 8, 1980

  - Michael George
    b. Feb. 18, 1955
    - Holly Dorothy
      b. Dec. 27, 1986
    - Colt Cedar

  - Thomas John
    b. Feb. 8, 1957

  - Donna Marie
    b. March 16, 1958
    m. Brown
    - Julia Ann
      b. July 5, 1982
    - Justine Marie
      b. May. 18, 1988

GENEALOGICAL CHART #4C
DESCENDANTS OF ADOLPH AND EMMA RAPP

THE LYDON BRANCH

Emma Mae Rapp
m. Robert Lydon

Michael
b. Sept. 13, 1946
m. Jan. 25, 1975
to Marlene Enders

Katey
b. April 11, 1976
Jeannie
b. Aug. 17, 1977
Michael
b. Dec. 21, 1978

Mary
b. June 18, 1955
m. July 25, 1978
to Todd Phoenix

Sarah
b. Sept. 16, 1985
Antonio
b. Sept. 4, 1993 (adopted)

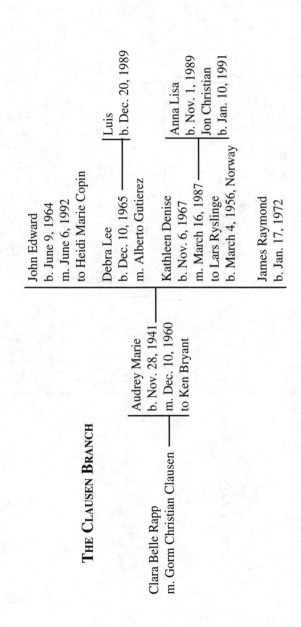

GENEALOGICAL CHART #4D

DESCENDANTS OF ADOLPH AND EMMA RAPP

THE CLAUSEN BRANCH

Clara Belle Rapp
m. Gorm Christian Clausen

Audrey Marie
b. Nov. 28, 1941
m. Dec. 10, 1960
to Ken Bryant

John Edward
b. June 9, 1964
m. June 6, 1992
to Heidi Marie Copin

Debra Lee
b. Dec. 10, 1965
m. Alberto Gutierez

Luis
b. Dec. 20, 1989

Kathleen Denise
b. Nov. 6, 1967
m. March 16, 1987
to Lars Ryslinge
b. March 4, 1956, Norway

Anna Lisa
b. Nov. 1, 1989
Jon Christian
b. Jan. 10, 1991

James Raymond
b. Jan. 17, 1972

GENEALOGICAL CHART #4E

DESCENDANTS OF ADOLPH AND EMMA RAPP

THE ADOLPH RAPP, JR. BRANCH

Adolph Rapp
m. Lorene White

- **Agnes Lorene** b. June 6, 1939, m. Jan. 28, 1972 to Dale Leistico
  - James Allen b. Nov. 13, 1973
  - Jonathan b. Jan. 13, 1974 (stillborn)
  - Laurene Elaine b. May 16, 1977
  - Susan Michelle b. July 22, 1979

- **Leo Adolphus** b. April 30, 1940, m. Feb. 8, 1969 to Nona Currier
  - Brian Leo b. July 26, 1972, m. Kimberly Upjohn
    - Collin b. March 3, 1994
  - Kevin Jon b. Jan. 4, 1974
  - Lorene Celeste b. April 12, 1979
  - Kathleen b. Sept. 22, 1986

- **David Francis** b. Nov. 26, 1944, m. June 10, 1967 to Sandy McCoy
  - Lisa Anne b. July 24, 1968, m. Mark Freitas
  - Timothy John b. Aug. 13, 1969, m. Trisha Travaglia
    - Garret Alexander b. Jan. 5, 1994
    - Amanda Marie b. Jan. 16, 1991
  - Christina Marie b. March 22, 1971, m. Colt Turner
    - Candice Linn b. June 26, 1993
  - Steven John b. Sept. 19, 1977
    - Hana Lee b. March 30, 1995

- **Arthur Samuel** b. Jan. 28, 1948, lived 10 days

- **Louis Francis** b. Oct. 21, 1950, m. Aug. 1, 1970 to Linda Baumer
  - Christopher Francis b. Jan. 22, 1972
  - Melissa Marie b. Dec. 23, 1972
  - Lisbeth Mary b. April 2, 1977

GENEALOGICAL CHART #4ғ
DESCENDANTS OF ADOLPH AND EMMA RAPP

THE KITZMILLER BRANCH

Mary Rapp
m. Owen Kitzmiller

Carl Owen
b. March 20, 1947
m. June 1, 1968
to Linda
b. March 20, 1949

Owen
b. Feb. 20, 1970
m. March 8, 1989
to Monica Navarro
d. May 14, 1995

Ron
b. Feb. 14, 1972

Danny
b. March 13, 1974

Daniel
b. Nov. 18, 1948
m. Jan. 17, 1972
to Cathy Anderson
b. June 30, 1950

John
b. April 8, 1974

David
b. Oct. 17, 1978

Susan
b. Oct. 31, 1950
m. Tom Vaughn

Frank
b. Oct. 15, 1959

GENEALOGICAL CHART #4G
DESCENDANTS OF ADOLPH AND EMMA RAPP

THE FRANK RAPP BRANCH

Frank Rapp
m. Patricia Wheatcraft

Patricia
b. Dec. 13, 1945

Kathleen
b. Sept. 14, 1948
m. June 27, 1976
to Robert Perlesweig

- Pesha
  b. Aug. 18, 1977
- David
  b. March 22, 1980

Margaret Mary (Meg)
b. Dec. 16, 1949
m. Feb. 4, 1984
to David Robinson

- Joseph
  b. Dec. 24, 1984
  - Aileen Elizabeth
    b. June 5, 1985
  - Corrine Terese
    b. July 16, 1990

Terese
b. April 9, 1952
m. Oct. 9, 1982
to Brian Hagerty

- Maria
  b. April 1, 1985

Mauré
b. Feb. 3, 1956
m. July 19, 1980
to Layne Howard

- Erin
  b. July 31, 1984
- Lauren
  b. April 21, 1987

Francine
b. June 8, 1961
m. Aug. 5, 1983
to David Armstrong

- Angela Grace
  b. March 6, 1984

GENEALOGICAL CHART #4H
DESCENDANTS OF ADOLPH AND EMMA RAPP

THE TARQUINIO BRANCH

Margaret Rapp
m. Amadeus Tarquinio

Laurence Francis ("Larry")
b. March 14, 1950
m. March 26, 1980
to Norma Jean Naylor
b. June 12, 1956

Andrew Morgan
b. Jan. 9, 1984

James Eric
b. Sept. 16, 1993

Douglas Timothy
b. Nov. 6, 1951

Kenneth Mark
b. March 7, 1953
m. April 26, 1987
to Claire Bueno
b. Oct. 13, 1960

Angelina Marie
b. Aug. 18, 1991

Sarah Elizabeth
b. Aug. 4, 1995

Steven Dominick
b. August 23, 1955
m. August 2, 1986
to Cheryl Weizel
b. Sept. 3, 1955

Brandon Forrest
b. Feb. 12, 1992

Janet Marie ("Alex")
b. June 23, 1964

MAMA'S PHILOSOPHY

Mama died in 1975, but many of the people who knew her throughout her long life still quote her platitudes, either consciously or unconsciously. Here are some example's of her philosophy:

"The more you stir a stink, the more a stink will stink."

"Rules are for fools."

"It is far better to pursue than to possess."

"Don't wash your dirty linen in public. If asked personal questions about the family, just say, 'I don't know.'"

"Don't brag about something you are going to do unless you are inviting that person along with you."[67]

On Questioning Others: "If they want you to know, they will tell you."

"Be careful as you travel down life's road," Mama said. "Each step you take helps determine which path you will choose when you come to the next fork in the road. That will influence how you live the rest of your life."

On Regrets: "No one can live their life without regrets. But try to live your life so you have as few as possible."

---

[67] I once learned that lesson the hard way. When I told my cousin Floyd I was going to a movie, Mama said, "No you aren't. Because Floyd can't go too. So you can't go either, now."

"Look up when you are down."

When trying to solve a dilemma, Mama always said, "There has to be a way!"

If something didn't work out, she said, "The time wasn't right."

"I'll think about it tomorrow!" (Mama was way ahead of Scarlett O'Hara on this one. She said this before the film "Gone With the Wind" was released.)

One thing she always stressed was to "count your blessings."